PHILOSOPHY IN THE SAMĀDHIRĀJASŪTRA

PHILOSOPHY IN THE SAMĀDHIRĀJASŪTRA

THREE CHAPTERS FROM
The Samādhirājasūtra

KONSTANTY RÉGAMEY

Foreword by
JACQUES MAY

MOTILAL BANARSIDASS PUBLISHERS
PRIVATE LIMITED • DELHI

First Published: *Warsaw, 1938*
First Indian Edition: *Delhi, 1990*

ISBN: 81-208-0763-4

Also available at:
MOTILAL BANARSIDASS
41 U.A., Bungalow Road, Jawahar Nagar, Delhi 110 007
120 Royapettah High Road, Mylapore, Madras 600 004
24 Race Course Road, Bangalore 560 001
Ashok Rajpath, Patna 800 004
Chowk, Varanasi 221 001

PRINTED IN INDIA
BY JAINENDRA PRAKASH JAIN AT SHRI JAINENDRA PRESS, A-45 NARAINA INDUSTRIAL AREA, PHASE I, NEW DELHI 110 028 AND PUBLISHED BY NARENDRA PRAKASH JAIN FOR MOTILAL BANARSIDASS PUBLISHERS PVT. LTD., BUNGALOW ROAD, JAWAHAR NAGAR, DELHI 110 007.

FOREWORD

Konstanty Régamey (1907-1982) was born in Kiev of a Swiss family which had emigrated to Russia in the 19th century. He fled from Russia to take refuge in Poland in 1917 and then subsequently from Poland to Switzerland in 1945. He had a double career, being both a musical composer and an orientalist. In the domain of orientalism, his preferred field was the language which Franklin Edgerton had termed "Buddhist Hybrid Sanskrit", and which was the vehicle for the canonical literature of Mahāyāna Buddhism in India.

K. Régamey's interest in this literature was not just linguistic, but also philosophical, as is most remarkably witnessed by his edition and translation of *Three Chapters from the Samādhirājasūtra*, first published in Warsaw in 1938 and now reprinted through the good offices of Motilal Banarsidass under the title, *Philosophy in the Samādhirājasūtra*. Originally, this work was the doctoral thesis of K. Régamey, a thesis defended at the University of Warsaw in 1936.

The *Samādhirājasūtra* is one of the essential canonical texts of Great Vehicle Buddhism. Dating from perhaps the second century A.D., it presents an early form of the doctrine of the void (*śūnyavāda*), one of the principal philosophical doctrines of the Mahāyāna. In this respect, the *sūtra* is of fundamental philosophical importance; it is, notably, of major authority for the Madhyamaka school, which is *śūnya-vāda* par excellence.

The three chapters (VIII, XIX and XXII) chosen by Régamey were not selected arbitrarily. Chapter VIII treats of the inexistence of *dharmas*; Chapter XIX of the identity of their essence; Chapter XXII treats of the nature of the bodies of the Buddha. These are all essential themes of the philosophy of the Great Vehicle and *śūnya-vāda*.

Even today, Régamey's work is the only one which treats the *Samādhirāja* with the rigour demanded, both in its textual critique and its linguistic and philosophical approaches. Régamey and his teacher, Stanislaw Schayer, had envisaged an edition of the whole *Samādhirāja*. But the project was cut short by the Second World War, and nothing more of it ever appeared apart from the three chapters chosen by Régamey. The editions of Dutt and Vaidya have the merit of presenting us with a complete text, but neither is critical. As for a translation, Jean Filliozat had worked on this task for a long time in his courses at the Ecole Pratique des hautes etudes in Paris; it seems that he may have left us a manuscript of an integral translation, but it remains unpublished to this day.

In Warsaw's destruction in 1944 everything of Régamey's work disappeared, manuscripts as well as the stocks of bookstores. Being a doctoral thesis, the *Three Chapters* had been sent around to some extent; nonetheless, it still remained difficult to find in bookstores. We see, then, the importance of the present reprinting, because of the rarity of the work and equally because of its interest for Mahāyānist Buddhist literature and thought.*

JACQUES MAY

---

*My thanks to Dr. Tom Tillemans for kindly having rendered my text into Eng..

CONTENTS

PREFACE.

Among the „9 Dharmas" of Nepal, *Samādhirājasūtra* is the only one of the greater texts which is less known and not completely edited as yet. It is rather surprising, considering that the text was very important, as testified by the numerous and extensive quotations in the later Buddhist literature. The *Samādhirājasūtra* is one of the most authoritative texts for Candrakīrti and Śāntideva, very often quoted in the works of these famous writers.

As Professor Stanislaw Schayer and myself intend to bring out an edition of the whole text, the present work is but preparatory, and presents as a specimen of the *Samādhirājasūtra* three philosophical chapters: VIII, XIX and XXII, giving an approximate idea of the doctrinal standpoint of the sūtra. It is obvious that these three chapters are not sufficient to convey all the characteristics of the entire sūtra. Consequently, I refrain from drawing any general and premature conclusions for the present, while analysing only the principal features of the above chapters. As our intended systematic edition will be accompanied by a volume containing the Sanskrit—Tibetan—Chinese indices, the present work will include but a list of Chinese words quoted in the text and an index of the most important terms.

The small size of the present work, however, allows me to give more attention to the Tibetan and Chinese versions, and to make greater use of the Commentary of *Mañjuśrīkīrti* on the *Samādhirājasūtra*. The same reason enables me to treat in detail the linguistic features of those chapters.

I avail myself of the opportunity to express my sincerest gratitude to Professor St. Schayer for the unceasing and the invaluable help which he was kind enough to render in the preparation of my work. The foot-notes of my book prove but very imperfectly how much I owe to Prof. Helmer Smith, and I can hardly miss this occasion in giving my sincerest thanks to him. It gives me also a great pleasure in acknowledging my indebtedness to Mademoiselle Marcelle Lalou and to Prof. Jan Jaworski who very kindly helped me in all the subjects concerned with Tibetan and Chinese respectively. My grateful thanks are due to all the persons whose suggestions allowed me to solve some difficult problems of my work, specially to Prof. Jean Przyluski and to Prof. Jules Bloch. Mr. Hiraṇmoy Ghoshal deserves my best thanks for having revised my English.

The acknowledgement of my indebtedness will not be complete unless I express my profound gratitude to the authorities of the Fundusz Kultury Narodowej and of the Kasa im. Mianowskiego without whose kind help this book would have remained unpublished.

Constantin Régamey.

LIST OF ABBREVIATIONS.

A.: The Sanskrit Ms. of the *Samādhirājasūtra*, fond sanskrits 144/145
B.: " " " " " " " " 143
C.: " " " " " " " " 146
Bibliothèque Nationale, Paris.

D.: The Sanskrit Ms. of the *Samādhirājasūtra*, Sanskrit Mss. Add. 916, University Library, Cambridge.

Ch.: The Chinese version of the *Samādhirājasūtra*, Taishō 639.

T.: The Tibetan version of the *Samādhirājasūtra*, which is preserved in two xylographs:

N.: The Narthang Edition, Mdo IX, fonds tib. 414 } Bibl. Nation.,
P.: The Peking Edition, Mdo XI, fonds tib. 72 } Paris.

K.: *Kīrtimala*, the Conmmentary of Mañjuśrīkīrti on the *Samādhirājasūtra* preserved in Tibetan version only: Mdo-'grel XXXVIII, fonds tib. 233, Bibl. Nat., Paris.

Pr.: *Prasannapadā* of Candrakīrti, Bibl. Buddhica, IV, St.-Petersburg, 1913.

S.: *Śikṣāsamuccaya* of Śāntideva, Bibl. Buddhica, I, St.-Petersburg, 1897 (1902).

c. T.: emendation according to the Tibetan version.
c.Ch.: " " " " Chinese version.
ad.: adds.
ins.: inserts.
om.: omits.

AK.: *Abhidharmakośa*, translation of Louis de La Vallée Poussin, Paris Louvain, 1923—31.

Aspects: Nalinaksha Dutt, *Aspects of Mahayana Buddhism*, London, 1930.

Ausgewählte Kapitel: St. Schayer, *Ausgewählte Kapitel aus der Prasannapadā*, Kraków 1931.
The Doctrine of Pr. P.: E. Obermiller, *The Doctrine of Prajñāpāramitā*, Acta Orientalla XI, 1932.
IHQ: *Indian Historical Quarterly*, Calcutta.
JRAS: *Journal of the Royal Asiatic Society*, London.
EB: *Eastern Buddhist.*
OLZ: *Orientalistische Literaturzeitung*, Leipzig.
Precanonical Buddhism: St. Schayer, *Precanonical Buddhism*, Archiv Orientalni, Prague, VII, 1935.
RO: *Rocznik Orientalistyczny*, Lwów.
Siddhi: Vijñaptimatratāsiddhi de Hiouan Tsang, tr. par Louis de la Vallée-Poussin, Paris, 1928—29.

INTRODUCTION.

1. GENERAL REMARKS.

The sources giving information about the *Samādhirājasūtra* till now, besides the Mss. were:

1) The edition of Śarat Chandra Das and Harimohan Vidyābhūṣaṇ in the „Buddhist Text Society" (Series 4), of which there appeared only the first fascicle (Calcutta, 1896) containing the chpts. I—XVI. It is an uncritical edition, does not correct the errors of the Ms. and contains a great number of false readings.

2) Quotations in the Buddhist Literature, especially in the *Prasannapadā* of Candrakīrti and in the *Śikṣāsamuccaya*[1]) of Śāntideva.

3) The summary given by Rajendralal Mitra in *The Sanskrit Buddhist Literature of Nepal*, Calcutta, 1882, p. 207—221.

---

[1]) In this text the *Samādhirājasūtra* is always quoted under the name *Candrapradīpa*. This title which is probably connected with the name of the Bodhisattva *Candraprabha*, the chief interlocutor of Buddha in our text, occurs also in the introductory stanzas of the *Samādhirājasūtra (candrapradīpam*,.. *sūtrarājam*, *candrapradīpam*.. *sūtrādhirājaṃ* etc.). Cf. the *Mañjuśrīmūlakalpa* p. 100, l. 26 where this title is quoted among the sacred texts which are to be, recited before a *paṭa: Āryaprajñāpāramitā Āryacandrapradīpasamādhim Āryadaśabhūmakaḥ Āryasuvarṇaprabhāsottamāḥ Āryamahāmāyūrī Āryaratnaketudhāriṇīṃ* (cf M. Lalou, *Iconographie des étoffes peintes*. Buddhica VI, Paris, 1930, p. 6, foot-note). According to the same *Mañjuśrīmūlakalpa*, before the making of a *maṇḍala* one must perform complicated rites and among other things the following texts must be read before the four doors symbolizing the cardinal points: the *Prajñāpāramitā* in the South, the *Candrapradīpasamādhi* in the West, the *Gaṇḍavyūha* in the North and the *Suvarṇaprabhāsa* in the East (cf. M. Lalou, *Trois aspects de la peinture bouddhique*, Annuaire de l'Inst. de Philologie et d'Histoire Orientales, t. III, Bruxelles 1935, p. 257). Cf. also the title of the Chinese version.

For the present edition I have made use of the following Mss.:

A. fonds sanskr. 144/145, chpt. VIII f. 29a—32a, chpt. XIX f. 79a—82a, chpt. XXII f. 91a—94a. Bibliothèque Nationale, Paris.
B. fonds sanskr. 143, chpt. VIII f. 19b—21a, chpt. XIX f. 55b—57b, chpt. XXII f. 60b—63a. Bibliothèque Nationale, Paris.
C. fonds sanskr. 146, chpt. VIII f. 40b—44b, chpt. XIX f. 102b—107a, chpt. XXII f. 113a—118b. Bibliothèque Nationale, Paris.
D. Sanskr. Ms. Add. 916, chpt. VIII f. 27b—30b, chpt. XIX f. 82b—86b, chpt. f. 91a—94b. University Library, Cambridge.

These are, unfortunately, late copies dating from the beginning of the XIXth century, and containing numerous mistakes. They can be divided into two groups. A and D which show a very close agreement, give the best readings; B and C also agree, but C contains a greater numbers of errors. All the four are written in Nepalese character, except C where, beginning from f. 167a, one finds a very fine *nāgarī*.

The division into chapters is identical in all the Mss. except for the last chapters. In my edition I have preserved the numbering of chpts as it was in the Mss., but have introduced my own division into §§. In the quotations the Roman and the Arabic figures indicate respectively the chpts and the §§.

I have made extensive use of the commentary on *Samādhirāja* of Mañjuśrīkīrti, entitled *Kīrtimala* and preserved in Tibetan version only: *'pags-pa-chos-thams-cad-kyi raṅ bźin-mñam-pa-ñid-rnam-par-spros-pa'i tiṅ ṅe-'dzin-gyi-rgyal-po źes bya-ba theg-pa chen-po'i mdo'i 'grel-pa grags-pa'i phreṅ-ba źes bya-ba*, Tanjur, Mdo-'grel XXXVIII (Cordier 233).

2. VERSIONS.

The Tibetan version of the *Samādhirājasūtra* is entitled: *'phags-pa-chos-thams-cad-kyi raṅ bźin-mñam-pa-ñid-rnam-par-spros-pa-tiṅ-ṅe-'dzin-gyi rgyal-po* (*ārya-sarva-dharma-svabhāva-samatā-vipañcita*[2])-*samādhi-rāja)* and is contained in the Mdo XI, 1 of the Peking (P) edition (Bibl. Nat., Paris, fonds tib. 72) and in the Mdo IX, 1 of the Narthang (N) edition (Bibl. Nat. fonds tib. 414). The N is follo-

[2]) And not °*tā* as is written by Feer, Annales du Musée Guimet, II, p. 249.

wed by the colophon: (f. 237b) *rgya·gar-gyi mkhan-po śu-len-dra-bodhi dań | żus-chen-gyi lo-tsā-ba ban-de dha-rma-tā-śī-las bsgyur-ciń żus-te | skad-gsar bcad-kyis kyań bcos-nas gtan-la pḣab-bo.* Hence the translators of the text were Śīlendrabodhi and Dharmatāśīla living in the IXth century A. D.

The Tibetan translation agrees very closely with the Sanskrit text, gives often better readings and sometimes fills up the gaps (e. g. XXII, 12). But the division into chapters and their numbering are not quite identical in both texts. To the chpts VIII and XIX of the original correspond respectively the VIIIth (P f. 21b—23 b, N f. 36b—40a) an the XIXth (P f. 71b—74b, N f. 108b—113a) chpts in the Tibetan, but the chpt. XXII of the Sanskrit text (*Tathāgatakāyanirdeśaparivartta)* is represented in the Tibetan version by two chpts.: the XXIInd *(lus-ńes-par-bstan-pa'i le'u,* P f. 78a—78b, N f. 118b - 119a) containing §§ 1—6, and the XXIIIrd *(de-bżin-gśegs-pa'i sku ńes-par-bstan-pa'i le'u,* P f. 78b—81a, N f. 119a—123a) corresponding to the §§ 7—54 of the XXIInd chpt. of the Sanskrit text. This Tibetan division is justified by the fact that only the §§ 7—54 deal with the Body of Tathāgata, while the initial §§ are concerned with the common human body. This difference is made obvious in Tibetan by the different rendering of the word *kāya.* The physical body is translated as *lus,* while both the Absolute and the Material Bodies of the Buddha are called *sku.*

Similarly, in the *Kīrtimala* two chpts correspond to the XXIInd chpt. of the Sanskrit text, but the division is different again. The first part (*chos-kyi sku'i le'u,* fonds tib. 233, f. 86b—88b) corresponds to the §§ 1—37 of the Sanskrit text, and the second part (*de-bżin-gśegs-pa'i sku ńes-par-bstan-pa'i le'u,* f. 88b—89b) to the rest of the chapter. The contents do not justify this division.

In order to avoid complications I use for the Tibetan version the numbering of the Sanskrit text. So, for instance, XXII, 10 corresponds, in the Tibetan text, to the second § of the XXIIIrd chpt.

Though the *Samādhirājasūtra* had not met with special recognition in the Far-East, and is rarely quoted by the Chinese commentators, there are three Chinese versions of this text: two partial and one complete. All the three have the title: *Yüeh teng san mei ching*= =*Candrapradīpasamādhisūtra*[3]). The complete version (Taishô 639)

---

[3]) Cf. the f. note 1.

made by Narendrayaśas A. D. 557, is divided into ten fascicles. The translation of the chpt. VIII is contained in the 2nd fscl. (Taishô 639 f. $556c_{ult}$—$557a_{27}$), the version of chpts. XIX and XXII in the 5th fscl. (Taishô 639, f. $574b_{1}$—$575a_{11}$ and f. $576a_{17}$—$577b_{24}$). Of the partial versions, one (Taishô 640) is attributed to *Shih-sien-kung* of the earlier Sung dynasty (A. D 420—479) and contains the translation of the 6th fscl. of the above-mentioned text. The other version (Taishô 641), according to the catalogues, contains the extracts from the chapters forming the 7th fscl. of the Narendrayasas' version. The colophon of the text mentions *An-shi-kao* (IInd century A. D.) as the translator. It is, however, very improbable because the majority of texts attributed to this translator are apocryphal.

As the two versions, just mentioned, do not contain the chapters here dealt with, we shall take into account the translation of Narendrayaśas alone. It differs essentially from the actual Sanskrit text, which fact helps us determine the development of the *Samādhirājasūtra* and its approximate date. On the evidence of the Tibetan version we may state that the *Samādhirājasūtra* existed in the IXth century in its actual form. The Chinese version of the earlier Sung dyn. (the presumed translation of *An-shi-kao* is left out of consideration, as its date remains to be ascertained) points out that there was already in the 5th century A. D. a text called *Candrapradīpasūtra* containing some chapters which agree with those of the *Samādhirāja*. As to the entire work, the earliest reliable evidence is given by the translation of Narendrayaśas, A. D. 557. It differs considerably from the Sanskrit and the Tibetan texts. In the following we shall examine only those differences which are to be found in the chpts. VIII, XIX and XXII.

Some disagreements, as e. g. the omission of the stereotyped formula, opening nearly every chapter in the Sanskrit text: *atha khalu Bhagavan Candraprabhaṃ Kumārabhūtaṃ āmantrayate sma: tasmāt tarhi...* etc., may result from the division of the Chinese version into fascicles, rendering the demarcation of chapters unnecessary. But, generally speaking, the Chinese text is abridged, and, compared to the Sanskrit original, it wants mainly the passages of a more speculative (e. g. VIII, 1—7) or explanatory nature (e. g. chpt. XXII where the §§ 1—3 are translated in two Chinese sentences, and the stanzas 4—6 are altogether missing). On the other hand, the enumerations in the style of the *Prajñāpāramitāsūtras*, the mythological and narrative passages (but even those often abridged) and the gāthās—in a word, the components having a more archaic character,—are conserved. Judging from those facts one might suppose that the Narendrayaśas' translation represents the original text, as it was in the beginning of the VIth century, and that the present size of the Sanskrit and Tibetan texts is due to the accumulation, between the VIth and IXth centuries, of new elements, partly ancient glosses and commentaries (see e. g. the XXII, 9 where nearly every epithet is followed by a synonym having the character of a gloss: *animittaḥ sarvanimittāpagato... apramāṇo apramāṇadharmo... adṛśyaś cakṣuḥpathasamatikrānto...* etc.).

This hypothesis, however, is contradicted by several facts. Precisely the passage XXII, 9—12, just mentioned, contains in the Chinese translation a much more copious list of epithets than the Sanskrit and Tibetan texts, and the order of these epithets is different. Besides, the quotations from the *Samādhirājasūtra* in the *Prasannapadā* and the *Śikṣāsamuccaya* agree very closely with the actual Sanskrit text, a fact which suggests that already in the VIIth century A. D. the *Samādhirājasūtra* attained its present form. It is unlikely that modifications, so important, could take place within the course of a century, while there was no change during the two centuries that followed. Further, in the chpt. VIII the Chinese translation omits the gāthās exactly those which are quoted very accurately by Candrakīrti. Consequently one is led to the conclusion that the Chinese text is either an abridged translation or it is based on a shorter recension of the *Samādhirājasūtra*[4]). In the following, slight divergencies between the original and the translations, arising from a difference of interpretation, are treated in the foot-notes.

Summing up, we may state that the *Samādhirājasūtra* was composed not later than the IVth century A. D., as proved by the Chinese translation of the earlier Sung. The internal evidences, above

---

[4]) The omission of gāthās in the VIIIth chpt. may be explained by the fact that these verses, contrary to the preserved gāthās of the XIXth and XXIInd. chpts, are nothing but a poetical paraphrase of the preceding prose narration. But in some other instances we are compelled to admit that there is a gap in the Ch. text, so e. g. XIX, 4—10, cf. the f. note 96.

all certain archaisms of the metaphysical topics (see chpt. 6 of the Introduction), allow us to place the text in the age of the *Prajñāpāramitāsūtras*[5]) and before that of the *Laṅkāvatāra*, i. e. in the IIIrd century, but direct proofs are wanting. Further, we may suppose that the *Samādhirājasūtra* in the VIIth century probably, and c e r t a i n l y in the IXth century attained its present size.

3. METRICS.

Metres.

In the chpts VIII, XIX, and XXII the following metres are used:

I. *Śloka* which is generally of the type *pathyā*. Occasionally other varieties of the *Śloka* are met with:

a) *rephavipulā*, in its most usual form ⏓ – ⏑ – | – ⏑ – ⏓ XXII, 22c, 28a, 33a, 42c (in this last case with the first syllable resolved),

b) *mavipulā* x x x x – – – ⏓, regularly with the end of the word after the fifth syllable: XXII, 16c, 18c, 20c, 21a, 29c, 35c, 36a, 37c, 45c.

c) *bhavipulā* x x x x – ⏑ ⏑ ⏓: the only one case XXII, 52c. For the verse VIII, 5a which contains only seven syllables, see the foot-note 51.

The even padas (b, d) are quite regular, except XXII, 22b. May we suppose here the scansion *talakṣaṇa?*

II. *Triṣṭubh* (*Indravajrā* and *Upendravajrā*). In the *Indravajrā* the initial syllable is resolved in: VIII, 7d, 25d, 26b, 27d, 28d, 31b. In VIII, 28c is resolved the fifth syllable. The verse VIII, 28d contains two resolved syllables: the first and the fifth. The fourth syllable of the *Upendravajrā* is resolved in VIII, 7b, c. This is a vasriety of the *Triṣṭubh* completely unknown in Pali and the earlier poetry, and seems to be an innovation of the Mahāyāna versifiers, ee the foot-note 53.

III. *Jagatī* (*Indravaṃśa* and *Vaṃśastha*). The *Indravaṃśa* in VIII, 24c, 27d has the first syllable resolved (°*jam* in the 27c is regarded as long, being at the end of a word).

IV. *Dodhaka* which is very regular, though this regularity is attained by means of a prosody much freer than in the more archaic

[5]) In the *Mañjuśrīmūlakalpa* the *Candrapradīpasamādhi* is quoted among the older Mahāyāna sūtras (cf. the f. note 1).

metres like the *Śloka* and the *Triṣṭubh-Jagatī*. The monotony of these identical verses is interrupted by XIX, 19b, d which constitute an interesting instance of the *Proto-dodhaka:* —◡—◡ | ⏖— | ◡◡— | ⏑̲, a very archaic Buddhist metre, cf. the foot-note 118. The verse XIX, 27a is quite irregular, the initial dactyl being replaced by *tathă*; the text seems to be corrupt, but it is attested in this form by all the Mss. and confirmed indirectly by the Tibetan and Chinese translations. Cf., however, the „apparatus" to this verse.

The following stanzas are formed of these metres [6]):

a) *Śloka*: VIII, 5, 6; XXII, 13—37, 40—54;

b) *Dodhakaṃ samavṛttam:* XIX 16—36; XXII, 4—6;

c) *Upajāti*: a quatrain composed of the *Triṣṭubh* and the *Jagatī* appearing in an unrestricted order, different in every stanza: VIII, 7; 21—31.

Prosody.

The regularity of some metres in the *Samādhirājasūtra* can be attained thanks to a flexible prosody based on the bilingual character of the „Buddhist" vernacular, which has for almost every long ending a corresponding short dialectical ending, e. g. *ă* for *ā*, *i* for *e*, *u* for *o* or *am* etc. (see the following chapter). To the same category of facts belongs the treatment of the groups of two consonants and the geminates which either constitute „position" or are treated as a single consonant. In this last case the prosody is based on the well known dialectical phonetic simplification which, however, is not manifested in spelling, and the prosody alone shows us that it is nothing but a fact of orthography. Thus, in cases like *tapană pratāpana* XIX, 20, *dharmăsvabhāvam* XIX, 27, *lokavidūnă jvaleti* XIX, 22, *paśyatĭ jñāna*° XIX, 22, *pravarttitŭ jñānam* XIX, 30 *mată jñātam* XIX, 27, and perhaps *tăllakṣaṇaḥ* XXII, 22b, properly speaking, *patāpana, sabhāva, jaleti, ñāna, ñāta* and *talakṣaṇa* are concerned. Cf. the vesre XIX, 22a where *utpādo* has the initial syllable short. It was probably pronounced as *ŭpādo* < **uppādo* < **utpādo*. For *upīḍa* XIX, 17, 18 see the foot-note 116.

---

[6]) For technical reasons the single verses are not printed separately, but punctuated by a *rekha* only.

The *visarga* and the *anusvara* are preserved when metre requires it, as e. g. *varnaḥ kāyena* XXII, 18, *imaṃ samādhim* VIII, 29, *avalaṃbiya* XXII, 13, in other cases they are omitted: *śāsana lokavidūna* XIX, 22, *mata* side by side with *śrutaṃ* XIX, 27.

As metrical anomalies are to be noted the cases like: *ānabhiramyāḥ* XIX, 20, *sūsukhitā* XIX, 28, 31, *sūpariśuddhe* XIX, 35, *vīmati* XIX, 35, *cajjino* = *ca jino* VIII, 28 etc.

The short syllable, when at the end of a word, can serve as long, e. g.: *virajám anuttaram* VIII, 27, *susukhám anubhonti* XIX, 28, *dukhám anubhonti* XIX, 33. Sometimes it is evidenced by spelling: *dukhām anubhonti* XIX, 20, *ratīm anubhūya* XIX, 26.

4. LANGUAGE.

In the *Samadhirājasūtra* we find the arrangement of language which is typical of the Northern Buddhist texts: in prose passages a relatively correct Sanskrit (except some lexical dialectisms as *vyāhāra*, *pūrvayoga* etc.), and in gāthās—the so called „mixed Sanskrit", the vernacular which was recently characterised by Prof. J. Bloch as follows [7]: „Ce sont là, non des tentatives infructueuses pour écrire le sanskrit, mais plutôt des efforts mal reglés pour donner une forme littéraire à une langue locale..." These efforts at the beginning gave rise to a mixture of languages where Prakrit form occurred side by side with pure Sanskrit ones. The process of sanskritising was probably much greater in spelling than in pronunciation, as is proved by the prosody of vowels before *pr-*, *sv-*, *jñ-* etc. (see p. 13). Nevertheless, some peculiarities of the vernacular as the endings *i* for *e*, *u* for *o* etc. were maintained even in writing, though we cannot ascertain whether this spelling really reflected the living pronunciation or it served only to represent the short *ĕ* and *ŏ* not existing in Indian alphabets [8]).

---

[7]) *L'indo-aryen du Véda aux temps modernes*, Paris, 1934, p. 9.

[8]) Some linguistic features, especially those found in the Ms. Dutreuil de Rhins where such *i* and *u* count as long, point out that a certain „assombrissement du timbre" was actually produced in the early Middle Indian before the shortening of final vowels (See J. Bloch, *L'indo-aryen...*, p. 42). However, in the *Samādhirājasūtra* and in other texts of that epoch the repartition of *e* and *i*, *o* and *u* is different. *i* and *u* occur only when a short vowel is wanted, and,

The *Samādhirājasūtra* belongs to the epoch when this rapprochement to the Sanskrit standard is so advanced that the dialectical forms are preserved only in cases where regular Sanskrit is metrically inadmissible. In all other cases, i. e. in prose and, in gāthās, wherever the metre allows it, we find, at least in the orthography,* the standard Sanskrit forms.

So, we have, according to the requirements of metre, the sandhi: *dharmāṇa abhāvu* VIII, 21, *jināna antike* VIII, 30, *Cakravāḍa api* XIX, 19, *varṣa acintiya* XIX, 24, *śrūtva adharma* XIX, 33, but *animittā alakṣaṇā* VIII, 5 and even *anutpannā 'niruddhāś ca* VIII, 5, *abhāvā 'nakṣarāḥ* VIII, 6; *buddhāna utpādo* XIX, 22, *pravrajitvāna imaṃ* VIII, 29, *sarvi abhāva°* VIII, 7, *kāyi asāriki* XXII, 5, *antu ubhe api* XIX, 32, but *nāmneti* VIII, 23, *smarāmy ahaṃ* VIII, 21, *sukhāny anubhonti* XIX, 21; *yo icchi* VIII, 7, *so imu* VIII, 28, *labhyate anto* XXII, 41, but *so 'bhāva°* VIII, 21, *kandarake 'bhiramanti* XIX, 28, and even *socyate* (*=sa ucyate*) VIII, 7 and *cali 'vaśye* XXII, 6.

Very frequent are the instances of the sandhi like: *parvat' aneke* XXI, 19, *caiv' avalambiya* XXII, 4, *vicarant' imu* XIX, 29, *bhont' imi* XIX, 30[9]). For *atītam-adhvanī* VIII, 21 cf. the foot-note 73

The internal sandhi generally conforms to the Sanskrit standard except the *visarga* which is always dropped (*dukha* passim, *nisvabhāva* XXII, 43 etc.). Sometimes, when metre requires it, exceptional forms like *cittautpādo* XXII, 43 are met with.

The following endings are clearly formed on the Middle Indian principles:

ă corresponding to the ending of the nom. plur. masc. *āḥ*;

vilakṣaṇa XIX, 16, *°gata*, *yamalokika*, *deva* XIX, 17, *acintiya*, *dharma* XIX, 18, *nara* XIX, 28, 31, 32, *śūnyaka dharma*

---

contrary to the cases noticeable in the *Mahāvastu*, *e* or *o* can never be scanned as short. Here, we are probably concerned with a conventional arrangement of spelling (not yet accomplished in *Mahāvastu*): the pronunciation of the endings both short and long could be dark, but in cases where the ending was long, the Sanskrit spelling *e* or *o* was preserved, and the darkening of colour was noted only in cases where metrical reasons rendered impossible the maintaining of the Sanskrit spelling.

9) Usually the identical vowels undergo elision, but cf. *nity'abudhāḥ* XXII, 4 and *śrūtv' imu* XIX, 33.

nirātmaka XIX, 30, *apriya*, *rata* XIX, 32, *pratiṣṭhita* XIX, 34, 35, *gṛdhra* XIX, 36, *cyuta* XXII, 6,

ă instead of *ān*, acc. plur. masc.:

varṣa acintiya XIX, 24,

ă instead of *ā*, nom. sing. fem.:

carya viśuddha XIX, 22[10]),

i for *e*

loc. sing.: *kalpi* VIII, 21, °*kandari śānti* XIX, 35, *pūtiki kāyi aśāśvati* XXII, 4, *jīviti* XXII, 4, 6, *kāyi asāriki jīviti* XXII, 5, *kāyi nirātmaki* XXII, 6, *cali* XXII, 6, but *nitye* XXII, 4, *śūnye* XXII, 6, °*kandarake* XIX, 28,

nom. plur. masc.:

imi XIX, 30, *yāvanti* (?) VIII, 25 (cf. the foot-note 79),

acc. plur. masc.:

sarvi VIII, 7, *eti* XIX, 32,

u for *o*

utpannu VIII, 21, *kṛtu* VIII, 22, *tāvantu... svaru* VIII, 25 (cf. the f. note 79), *abhirūpu prasādiku* VIII, 26, *dharmu* XIX, 23, *nirvṛtu nāyaku* XIX, 23, *dṛṣṭu tathāgatu pūjitu* XIX, 25, *toṣitu mānasu* XIX, 25, *parigrahu* XIX, 29, *bhāvitu mārgu* XIX, 30, *nirjātu* XXII, 14, *saṃbhāvu* XXII, 17, *śāntu* XXII, 23, *kāyu* XXII, 29, 34, 54, *jñātu* XXII, 31, *sarvaśu* XXII, 29, but: *dṛṣṭo* XXII, 18, *kāyo* XXII, 20, 21, 30 etc. in places which are metrically indifferent.

u for *am*

acc. sing. masc.:

abhāvu VIII, 22, 23, *āśayu* VIII, 28, *imu* VIII, 28, XIX, 27, 29[11]), 33, *kālu* XIX, 24, *nirdeśu* XXII, 35, 37;

---

[10]) The same shortening in *tathă* XIX, 18, 27.

[11]) *imu* represents here naturally *imam* and not *ime* as suggested by B e n d a l l, *Śikṣāsamuccaya*, p. 194.

nom. acc. sing. neutr.:

pravarttitu XIX, 30, *dukhu* XIX, 32, *cittu* XXII, 26, *dṛṣṭu* XIX, 27, *ciru* XIX, 24, but *imam* XXII, 13, *udāram* XXII, 26 etc.

u for *au*

antu XIX, 32 (acc. dual. masc.?).

loc. sing, *asmi(n)*[12]):

śāsanasmin VIII, 28, °*kālasmi* VIII, 31, °*pathasmi* XIX, 17, *bodhivaṭasmi* XXII, 5, *nāmarūpasmi* XXII, 26, 27, cf. *ekahi* (<**ekaṃhi*<*ekasmi?)* XIX, 16,

nom. acc. plur. neutr. *ā*

tādṛśā, yādṛśā lakṣaṇā XXII, 15, *balā* XXII, 16; also often shortened: *kṣetră, tāttakă* XIX, 16, *yojană* XIX, 21,

acc. plul. fem of the *i*-stems *yaḥ*

koṭyo XXII, 23 (normal also in prose: VIII, 16, etc.)

gen. plur. *āna*

dharmāṇa VIII, 22, 24, *kalpāna* VIII, 29, *jināna* VIII, 30, *marutāna* XIX, 21, *buddhāna* XIX, 22, but *buddhānāṃ* XXII, 17, 19, 54. Cf. also *lokavidūna* XIX, 22,

instr. plur. *ehi*

lakṣaṇehi XXII, 19, *bhāvehi* XXII, 30, etc. and

the loc. plur. with long *ī* and *ū* side by side with the Sanskrit forms

ratiṣu XIX, 21, *dhātūṣu* XXII, 40,

on the contrary, the gen. plur. may contain a short wovel

°*koṭinam* VIII, 31 [13]).

---

[12]) As for the frequent endings *esmin*, I consider them, following Sénart (*Mahāvastu*, Paris, 1882, vol. I, p. XVII) as erroneus and awkwardly sanskritised forms. I have corrected them into *asmin* in every case.

[13]) We are concerned here with the Middle Indian system of double forms which may be used optionally. Prof. Helmer Smith compares the following Pali instances: *Kurūnaṃ* J. VI, 272[33]: *Kurūnaṃ* ib. 260[22]; *jātīsu* Suttanipāta 607a: *jātīsu* ib. 610f etc., and considers these double forms as resulting frcm the confusion of the masc. *-i*: *-in* and fem. *-i*: *-ī* stems.

Note also the following noun-forms:

samādhiya XIX, 27 (see the f. note 132), *Namucisya* XIX, 36 (gen. sing.), °*nadīye* XIX, 16 (loc. or gen. sing.), *mātāṃ* VIII, 7 (acc. sing. of *mātar*).

Under pronouns we find a still greater diversity of forms:

ettaka XXII, 21, *ettakā* XXII, 41, *tāttaka* XIX, 16, *yāttika* XIX, 16, *tahi* VIII, 25 (=*tasmin* or rather an adverbial form like Pali *tahiṃ*), *teṣa* XIX, 6, 35, *tehi* XIX, 32, XXII, 30, *yeṣa* XXII, 5, *kaści* VIII, 25, *kahiñcit* XIX, 28, 29, *keṣaci* XIX, 25 but, *keṣacid* XIX, 24, *sarveṣa* VIII, 30 and *sarvāṇa* VIII, 22, 24.

The verb betrays many characteristic Middle Indian features:

the Imperative, 2nd pers. plur. uses the 2nd pers. of the Indicative: *vijānatha* VIII, 5,

final consonants are dropped (but only where metre requires it): *icchi* (=*icchet*) VIII, 7, *pramumocu* VIII, 23 and the Aorist ending *ī*,

a frequent use of Aorists, which in prose have the regular Sanskrit forms; in the gāthās prevails the *-iṣ-* Aorist where in the ending of the 3rd pers. sing. *īt*, the *t* is dropped in conformity with the preceding point: *deśayī* VIII, 22, *upagamī* VIII, 26, *pravrajī* VIII, 28, *ārāgayī*, *bhāvayī* VIII, 30. This form should not be confused with the regular Sanskrit Passive Aorist *udapādi* which occurs in prose (VIII, 8, 10, 17). Note the sibilant Aorist *kurviṣu* XXII, 4 (cf. the f. note 147). and *prabudhyiṣu*(?)see the f. note 149) XXII, 5,

forms like: *jānāti* VIII, 6, *parāhananti* XIX, 9,

the Past Passive Participle: *janita* XXII, 24 (from *jan*- To be distinguished from the forms like the Infinitive *jānitum* XXII, 13, 45 from *jñā*-), *vijñapta* VIII, 9, *nirjita* XXII, 34 (probably resulting from *nirjāta* confused with *nirmita*, cf. the f. note 206).

gerunds in *-ya* (chiefly *-iya*) are rather seldom: *avalambiya* XXII, 4, even *kṛtya* VIII, 27; usually both simple as compound verbs have *-tvă* or *tvăna*. The quantity depends on the metre, thus: *dhāritvă*, *vācitvă* VIII, 29, but *paryāpuṇitvā* VIII, 29;

karitvāna XXII, 4, *nihanitvāna* XXII, 5, but *pravrajitvāna* VIII, 29. Note *sthihitvā* VIII, 22.

The verb *bhū-* has the following dialectical forms: Present, 3rd pers. sing. *bhoti* XXII, 22, 27, 30, 3rd pers. plur. *bhonti* XIX, 30, 34; Future, 3rd pers. sing. *bheṣyati* VIII, 24, XXII, 36; Aorist, 3rd pers. sing. *abhu* VIII, 26, 31. Note the medial form *bhaveta* XIX, 27.

The indeclinables too, according to the requirements of metre, oscillate between the Sanskrit and the Middle Indian forms: *sadă* VIII, 26, 30, XIX, 28, 31, 34, 36; *puna* XXII, 6; *vă* XIX, 29. *iti* has chiefly the Sanskrit form, but we also meet with forms like *supino ti* XIX, 26. Similarly, side by side with *api* XIX, 19 occurs *kṣetra pi* XIX, 16. In many cases the sandhi does not permit us to ascertain whether *api* (*'pi*) or *pi* is concerned, e. g. *nairayikāpi* XIX, 17, *no pi ca* (*no 'pi ca ?*) XIX, 17, 18 etc. Note the use of *nu* in the function of *nūnam* XIX, 12, 14, see the f. note 101.

Lexicology. In the chpts VIII, XIX, and XXII the following words deserve mention on account of their dialectical form or special meaning: *supino* XIX, 26, 27 (but *svapna*⁰ XXII, 6), *upīḍa* XIX, 17, 18, *avaśya* XXII, 6 (see the f. note 150), *vyāhāra* XXII, 11, *ānuśaṃsa* (see the f. note 90), *udāra* XXII, 26 (=Pāli *oḷārika*).

5. ORTHOGRAPHY.

The actual form of the text is the resultant of the dialectical modifications, orthographical usages of the Nepalese scribes and of their mistakes. It is not easy to distinguish those different strata. The most reliable help is supplied by the prose passages which contain generally a correct Sanskrit. Therefore, all the irregularities occurring in those passages may be safely considered as purely orthographical facts. So, the endings like the acc. plur. masc. *-āṃ* do not reflect, as it was supposed by Sénart[14]), the dialectical pronunciation, but result only from the usage of the scribes, as well as the contrary use of *n* instead of the *anusvara* in *mānsa* etc.

In fact, one could maintain even these orthographical usages in accordance with the late Prof. Sylvain Lévi who said[15]): „La tra-

[14]) *Mahāvastu*, vol. I, p. XIV, XVI.

[15]) *Mahāyāna Sūtrâlaṃkāra*, Paris, 1907, vol. I, p. II, III.

dition des scribes népalais a ses usages constants... et pour les textes qu'ils sont seuls à nous avoir conservés, il me paraît préférable de se conformer à leurs usages plutôt que de leur imposer les rigueurs d'un purisme théorique. Le sanskrit a bien assez d'uniformité pour qu'on n'aille pas effacer de parti pris les rares particularités de temps ou de lieu qui ont pu y marquer leur empreinte". But these words are concerned with the text preserved in one single Ms. And in cases when there are several Mss., the matter is not so simple. The spelling of diverse Mss. is so divergent and inconsequent, that any attempt to preserve the peculiarities of the „Nepalese orthographical tratidion" is impossible. Therefore, for the sake of uniformity, I am introducing in those cases the regular Sanskrit forms, which are, besides, almost always attested by at least one Ms. Consequently spellings like *rṇṇa, rmma, ryya. rvva* etc.[16]) are not maintained and the only Nepalese orthographical usage which I have adopted is the spelling *satva, bodhisatva, mahāsatva,* the spelling of words which are never written otherwise in the Nepalese Mss.[17]).

Of course, not all the irregularities are due to orthographical usages. Most of them are simple mistakes which have two sources: the resemblance of some letters and ligatures in the Nepalese writing: (*c* and *v, r* and *n, ṅ* and *ḍ, p* and *y, m* and *s, tya* and *bhya, kṣa* and *hu, śu* and *ṇḍa, tt* and *nt,* etc.[18]) and the similarity of certain sounds in later pronunciation: *b* and *v* (which are not distinguished in spelling), *r* and *l, n* and *ṇ, s* and *ś* or *ṣ*. Though these phonetical confusions cannot be imputed only to the ignorance of scribes, and may reflect some dialectical facts, they are preserved in so divergent forms in different Mss., that, here too, the introducing of the classical Sanskrit spelling was inevitable.

Our Mss. betray a still greater incongruency in the sandhi where the irregularities, in prose passages[19]), are obviously due to the incompetence of scribes. Therefore, here too, I am introducing regular forms, except in enumerations where some constant usages,

---

[16]) But I distinguish *rta* and *rtta,* this difference having some importance for the meaning.

[17]) See Sénart, *Mahāvastu,* vol. I, p. XVII, f. note.

[18]) Cf. Lefmann, *Zum Gathadialekt,* ZDMG, 29, 1875, pp. 221—223 and Sénart, *Mahāvastu,* vol. I, p. XII.

[19]) For the sandhi in gāthās see the preceding chapter.

common to all the Mss., as e. g. the preserving of *a* after *o* (*apramāṇo acintyo animitto*) seem to have the purpose of avoiding ambiguity which could result from the dropping of the negative *a*.

In order not to make the „apparatus" too cumbrous, I have not mentioned in the foot-notes all the irregularities which are concerned with orthography alone. In the Tibetan text I have pointed out only the most important „various readings". As for the Chinese text, since it is edited in Taishô, I have not indicated the various readings at all. In some instances, however, I was obliged to admit other readings than those adopted by the Taishô editors. In those cases I have mentioned it in the foot-notes under the translation.

6. CONTENTS. THE DOCTRINAL STANDPOINT.

The *Samādhirājasūtra* belongs to the group of texts called *vyākaraṇa* and contains, in conformity with this denomination, the explanations of different *samādhis* illustrated by stories meant to show the results of these meditations. But in no case can the present text be considered as a manual of trances. There is no mention of the technical methods of concentration. The word *samādhi* denotes in our text rather the subject of the concentration, a verbal formula to be meditated upon. The fundamental *samādhi* embracing in a certain measure all the remaining meditations, identified with the Mother-Prajñāpāramitā (VIII, 7), and giving the title to the entire work, is the „King of Samādhis" defined as „the thesis of the equality of all the dharmas in their essence" (*sarvadharmasvabhāvasamatāvipañcitasamādhirāja*). This thesis is developed in our text in its various aspects and formulated in different verbal redactions. The fact that w o r d s have the chief importance, is proved by the stereotyped recommendation occurring almost in every chapter,—a recommendation to read this *samādhi*, recite it, learn it by heart, etc.[20]). This „developing" of the thesis of equality is by no means a philosophical analysis of it. Quite on the contrary, this thesis is repeated dogmatically, illustrated by various details, and applied mechanically to

---

[20]) See, above all, XXII, 8. The term *samādhi* may be understood as the ensemble of all the varieties of the principal *samādhi*. In the Ch. translation it is said expressly: „he must learn, bear in mind, etc... that *samādhisūtra* (*san mei ching tien*)".

different facts, so that the samādhi-formula is often treated as a *dhāraṇī*. This manner of „explaining" is probably denoted by the term *vipañcita* in which there are joined two notions: the primitive meaning of the verb *vipañcayati* „to diffuse, to expand" and the sense of „explaining" attested by the Chinese rendering of this word: *yen shuo* = *vyākhyāna, nirdeśa* (cf. the foot-note 92 and Rosenberg, *Introduction to the Study of Buddhism*, Part I, *Vocabulary*, Tokyo 1916, p. 300)[21]).

Consequently the theses of the *Samādhirājasūtra* which have a doctrinal importance are for the most part independent of the principal samādhi-subject. They mostly result from the conceptions loosely joined with the fundamental topics and are concerned with some collateral subjects of meditation, as e. g. the non-existence of the dharmas (VIIIth chpt.), the nature of the Bodies of Buddha (XXIInd chpt.) etc. They are often contained in the gāthās, the subjects of which are much freer and consequently richer than those of the prose. They reflect some current ideas of the epoch and for that reason are of great importance to the reconstruction of the early Mahāyāna doctrine.

The chapters which I am editing in the present work, are precisely concerned with such „collateral conceptions" and, though they cannot give a sufficient idea of the standpoint of the entire sūtra, they may, nevertheless, supply some valuable points for the religious and philosophical history of that early epoch. The exact interpretation of certain conceptions of our text is not easy, because the prose passages have a dogmatic character, neglecting all reasonings, and the gāthās are often too laconic. The help of the Commentary is not always reliable, as there is a certain difference between the doctrine of the text and the philosophical standpoint of Mañjuśrīkīrti. The latter in his *Kīrtimala* seems to represent the classical *vijñānavāda* point of view with the theory of three *lakṣaṇas*, of the Triple Body etc., while the *Samādhirājasūtra* itself may not be as easily fitted into the frame of that idealistic school in its elaborated form.

---

[21]) Cf. Stede's, *Pali Dictionary*, s.v. *vipañcita*, where it is said on the authority of the Commentary on the *Suttanipāta*, 163, that *vipañcitaññu* is applied to those „who need a detailed instruction; thus learning by diffuseness".

The *Samādhirājasūtra* is one of the most authoritative texts not of the Yogācaras but of the Mādhyamikas. There we find the characteristic features of the so called „Doctrine of Prajñā-pāramitā" which formed, according to the Tibetan historiographers, the second „Swinging of the Wheel of the Doctrine" [22]) and which was characterised by the teaching about the absence of a real essence of all the dharmas. This conception is expounded in the VIIIth chpt. of our text and the epithets of the *dharmas* in the same chpt. (§ 2) as well as the definition of the *dharmakāya* supply other instances characteristic of that doctrine found especially in the *Prajñāpāramitāsūtras* and described by Stcherbatsky as „Relativitäts-Lehre".

Also the theory of the Bodies of Buddha is in the *Samādhirājasūtra* akin to the conceptions of the *Prajñāpāramitāsūtras*. Our text knows only two bodies: the *rūpakāya* and the *dharmakāya* (XXII, 7 and 34). The complicated theories concerning three or more bodies of Buddha and relying upon the speculations of the school of Maitreya-Asaṅga about the three aspects of reality, do not yet exist. The stress is laid not so much upon the fact that there are two bodies of Buddha, but upon the opposition between the real *dharmakāya*=the Absolute, and the imaginary, illusory *rūpakāya*, a phantom created by the magical power of the Buddha. A similar standpoint is to be found in the *Aṣṭasāhasrikā Prajñāpāramitāsūtra* [23]) which knows but two bodies, the *rūpakāya* and the *dharmakāya*. The latter is conceived of in two senses: 1) as the collection *(nikāya)* of *dharmas*, i. e. practices which make a being a Buddha (cf. XXII, 49 *aprameyā hi te dharmāḥ kalpakoṭyo niṣevitāḥ... tena acintyaḥ* [*me*] *kāyo*; it is the interpretation inherited from the Hīnayānists, cf. AK, VI, 67, according to which the *dharmakāya* is the collection of the *buddhakārakā dharmāḥ)*, and 2) as the Absolute (which is, contrary to the appearance, an older, protocanonical conception [24]).

The same two bodies are distinguished in the Chinese *Pari-*

---

[22]) See E. Obermiller, *Bu-ston*, I, 30 ff., *The Doctrine of Pr. P.* p. 91, Th. Stcherbatsky, *Die drei Richtungen in der Philosophie des Buddhismus*, RO, X, 1934, p. 9, 10.

[23]) *Aspects*, p. 96.

[24]) See *Precanonical Buddhism*, pp. 126—130 and A. B. Keith, IHQ, XII, 1, 1936, pp. 1—20.

nirvāṇasūtra[25]) and by Nāgārjuna in the *Mahāprajñāpāramitāśāstra*[26]). Cf. the *Vajracchedika*, p. 43[27]) and the *Suvarṇaprabhāsa*, where the chapter concerning the Triple Body is to be found in the later Chinese translations of I-tsing and Paramārtha, but is missing in the earliest translation of Dharmarakṣa[28]).

In this early epoch the nature of these two bodies is not yet strictly defined. In the *Samādhirājasūtra* we do not find the exact notion of the *nirmāṇakāya* of later texts, the phantom having no real existence, but possessing all the qualities of an ordinary man, born of parents and subject to human frailties. In the conception of the *rūpakāya* of the *Samādhirājasūtra* we find features which in the later texts characterise both the *nirmāṇa-* and the *sambhogakāya*. It is not the real body of Buddha, nor should one conceive the Buddha under its aspect (XXII, 7, 34). It has been created by the Buddha (XXII, 18, 19) in order to be visible for gods and men, it possesses the 32 marks of the Mahāpuruṣa (XXII, 15, 19), but its appearance is far from resembling a man. It is an effulgent being, full of splendour and majesty, reminding one of the *Prakṛtyātmabhava* of the *Prajñāpāramitāsūtras*[29]) and hard to be conceived by men. Although it possesses colours and marks (*guṇa, varṇa*), they are immeasurable (XXII, 38—45) and have no fit comparison (XXII, 40—44). Therefore it is possible to say about this body as much as about the *dharmakāya*, that it is practically inconceivable (XXII, 38, 39), the number of its marks being infinite. The contrast with the *dharmakāya* consists in that the latter is inconceivable in its very essence, has no marks at all (XXII, 15, 16, 33, 46), is undifferentiated (XXII, 14), immeasurable (XXII, 21, 46), unknowable (XXII, 17, 46, 48—52), and can be cognized only by means of the *samādhi* (XXII, 13, cf. the f.-note 155). It possesses all the features of the Mahāyānistic Absolute (XXII, 9—12).

It is, however, to be noted that also the *dharmakāya* of the *Samādhirājasūtra* shares some features with the *sambhogakāya* of the later Mahāyāna: it is born of immeasurable merits (XXII, 9, 14;

---

25) See EB, II, p. 21.

26) *Aspects*, p. 114.

27) See the foot-note 207 and *Precanonical Buddhism*, p. 126.

28) See D. T. Suzuki, *Studies on Laṅkāvatāra*, London, 1930, p. 311 Idzumi, edition of the *Suvarṇaprabhāsa*, Kyoto, 1936, p. XIV.

29) *Aspects*, p. 118, 119.

which is, according to the *Lankāvatāra* p. 28, 34[30]) the mark of the *Niṣyandabuddha*), and it is radiant (XXII, 14, 22, 49). This last feature is connected with the conception of the *citta prabhāsvara* which will be treated below.

It would be, on the other hand, very incorrect to infer from this doctrinal resemblance to the *Prajñāpāramitāsūtras* that the *Samādhirājasūtra* represents a radical *śūnyavāda*. The thesis of the equality of all the dharmas is interpreted rather in an idealistic sense. The commentator identifies the point of the hair which contains the entire Universe (XIX, 16) with the *citta*, and to a certain extent, we may consider that interpretation of an old mythological image as not distorting the intentions of the text[31]). The idealistic point of view is more evident in XXII, 25—27 where it is said that *nāmarūpa=citta*, because both the *nāmarūpa* and e. g. the *saṃjñā* are derived from the pure consciousness[32]). Cf. the *Yuktiṣaṣṭikā*[33]) where *rūpa* and *vijñāna* are identified.

Such conceptions met with already in very old strata of Buddhism[34]), suppose the treatment of the consciousness as a unique, fundamental, eternal element, the so called *ādiśuddha, prabhāsvara ekacitta* out of which are derived all the other elements. This doctrine can be found in the texts which, according to the scheme of the three Swingings of the Wheel, might represent the pure *śūnyavāda*, viz. the *Avataṃsaka*, the *Śrīmālādevīsiṃhanandasūtra*, the *Vimalakīrtinirdeśa* etc.[35]). Cf. the hymn of Nāgārjuna *Dharmadhātustotra*[36]) where the *dharmakāya* and the *dharmadhātu* are identified with the *citta prabhāsvara*.

This theory is expressly expounded in the *Samādhirājasūtra*: the Body of the Tathāgata is identified with the intellect (*buddhi*)

---

[30]) *Aspects*, p. 120.

[31]) Cf. the foot-note 112. In this passage only the stanza XIX, 30 interpretes the „equality" in a negativistic sense: *śūnyaka dharma nirātmaka sarve*. But the conception that all the dharmas are identical because they all are equally *nirātmaka*, is to be found also in later Yogācara texts, e. g. *Sūtrālaṃkara*, p. 94.

[32]) See the foot-note 202.

[33]) Yamaguchi, EB, 1926, VI, 1, p. 57ff.

[34]) E. g. *Ṣaḍdhātusūtra*, see *Precanonical Buddhism*, p. 125.

[35]) Cf. Sidhi, p. 109; Schayer, *Das mahāyānistische Absolutum*, OLZ, Juli 1935, col. 405, 406.

[36]) Taishō .675.

born of immeasurable merits (XXII, cf. the f.-note 157) and its features agree with those of the *citta ādiśuddha*. It is pure (*śuddha* XXII, 14), placeless (*aniketa* XXII, 10), steadfast (*dhruva* XXII, 10), motionless (*acala* XXII, 9=free from the *spandana* [37]). The effulgence of the *dharmakāya* (see p. 25) is explained by the fact that it is the *citta prabhāsvara*. The practice of the *samādhi* purifies the consciousness of the *kleśas* (XXII, 23, 24, 25—29, see the foot-note 202) and leads it to the state of a radiant, non-individual, psychical Substance: *cittam prabhāsvaram agṛddham nāmarūpasmi* (XXII, 27 cf. also XXII, 22).

We meet with a similar conception as early as in the Pali canon: Aṅg. Nik. I, 10 *pabhassaram idaṃ cittaṃ taṃ ca kho āgantukehi upakilesehi upakiliṭṭham* [38]. The epithets of the *dharmakāya* such as *acintyanidarśana* (XXII, 38), *aparyanta* (XXII, 12) and *cittam prabhāsvaram* strikingly remind one of the famous description of the Nirvāṇa in Dīgh. Nik. I, 223: *viññānaṃ anidassanaṃ anantaṃ sabbato pabham* [39]).

Thus we see that the *Samādhirājasūtra* does not represent either a radical *śūnyavāda* or a developed *vijñānavāda* and that it cannot be fitted into any period of the „Three Swingings". As we have similar difficulties with the classification of the texts such as *Avataṃsaka. Śrīmālādevīsūtra* etc., we should rather admit that this threefold scheme is too rigid and represents the historical facts but very inexactly. The data contained in those texts, including the *Samādhirājasūtra*, lead us to suppose that the early Mahāyāna was characterised by a metaphysical standpoint, common to all Mahāyāna schools, and having its roots in the old protocanonical strata, a standpoint which connected the negativistic *śūnyavāda* with a positive-idealistic conception of the *dharmakāya* = *dharmadhātu* = *citta prabhāsvara* [40]). In the present state of research we cannot determine this standpoint in detail, as yet. That will depend on the results of a further research on those texts, most of which remain to be edited.

---

[37]) See Schayer, *Das mah. Absolutum*, col. 407, 408.

[38]) *Precanonical Buddhism*, p. 131.

[39]) *Aspects*, p. 148.

[40]) Schayer, *Das mah. Absolutum*, col. 405.

SANSKRIT AND TIBETAN TEXTS

VIII.

1) tatra Bhagavān punar api[1] Candraprabhaṃ Kumārabhūtam āmantrayate sma: tasmāt tarhi Kumāra bodhisatvena mahāsatvenemaṃ samādhim ākāṃkṣatā kṣipraṃ cânuttarāṃ[2] samyaksaṃbodhim abhisaṃboddhukāmena sarvadharmāṇām abhāvasvabhāvajñānakuśalena bhavitavyam.

2) kathaṃ ca kumāra bodhisatvo mahāsatvaḥ sarvadharmāṇām[3]) abhāvasvabhāvajñānakuśalo bhavati. iha kumāra[4]) bodhisatvena mahāsatvena abhāvasvabhāvā[5]) animittā alakṣaṇā anutpannā aniruddhā[6]) anakṣarāḥ śūnyā ādiśāntāḥ prakṛtiviśuddhāḥ sarvadharmāḥ prajñātavyāḥ. yadā ca kumāra bodhisatvena mahāsatvena abhāvasvabhāvā . . . . prakṛtiviśuddhāḥ sarvadharmāḥ parijñātā bhavanti[7]) yathābhūtatas[8]) tadâyaṃ kumāra bodhisatvo mahāsatvaḥ sarva-

VIII.

//de-nas yaṅ bcom-ldan-'das-kyis zla-'od-gźon-nur-gyur-pa-la bka' stsal-pa/gźon-nu de-lta-bas-na byaṅ-chub-sems-dpa' sems-dpa'chen-po tiṅ-ṅe-'dzin 'di 'dod-ciṅ/myur-du bla-na-med-pa yaṅ-dag-par-rdzogs-pa'i byaṅ-chub mṅon-par-rdzogs-par-'tshaṅ-rgya-bar 'dod-pas chos thams-cad-kyi dṅos-po-med-pa'i ṅo-bo-ñid-kyi ye-śes-la mkhas-par bya'o//

//gźon-nu ji-ltar-na byaṅ-chub-sems-dpa' sems-dpa'-chen-po chos thams-cad-kyi dṅos-po-med-pa'i ṅo-bo-ṅid-kyi ye-śes la mkhas-pa yin źe-na/gźon-nu 'di-la byaṅ-chub-sems-dpa' sems-dpa'-chen-pos chos thams-cad dṅos-po-med-pa / ṅo-bo-ñid-med-pa/mtshan-ma-med-pa / mtshan-ñid-med-pa / ma-skyes-pa / ma-'gags-pa / yi-ge-med-pa/stoṅ-pa / gzod-ma-nas źi-ba / raṅ-bźin-gyis rnam-par-dag-pa yin-par rab-tu-śes-par bya'o / gźon-nu byaṅ-chub-sems-dpa' sems-dpa'-chen-pos nam chos thams-cad dṅos-

---

1) B puna pi. 2) C ākāṃkṣatā kṣimaṃ samādhim ākāṃkṣatā kṣiprañ cānut taraṃ. 3) C *ad.* ev'. 4) A °ro. 5) C abhāvā asvabhāvāḥ. 6) B °ddhā. 7) B bhavati. 8) C °taḥ.

dharmāṇām abhāvasvabhāvajñānakuśala ity ucyate.

3) sarvadharmāṇām abhāvasvabhāvajñānakuśalo hi kumāra bodhisatvo mahāsatvaḥ sarva [1])-r ūpa-śabda [2])-gandha-rasa-spraṣṭavya-dharmebhyo na rajyate [3]) na duṣyate [4]) na [5]) muhyate [6]). tat kasya hetoḥ? tathā hi sa taṃ dharmaṃ [7]) na samanupaśyati taṃ dharmaṃ [8]) nopalabhate [9]).

4) yo rajyeta, yatra [10]) va rajyeta, yena vā rajyeta; yo [11]) duṣyeta [12]), yatra vā duṣyeta [13]), yena vā duṣyeta [14]); yo muhyeta, yatra [10]) vā muhyeta, yena vā muhyeta, sa taṃ dharmaṃ na [15]) samanupaśyati, sa taṃ dharmaṃ [16]) nopalabhate [9]). taṃ dharmam asamanupaśyann anupalabhamānaḥ sarvatraidhātukenânadhyavasito [17]) bhavati, kṣipram imaṃ samādhiṃ pratilabhate, ksiprañ

po-med-pa / ṅo-bo-ñid-med-pa / . . . . / raṅ-bźin-gyis rnam-par-dag-pa yin-par rab-tu-śes-par-gyur-pa de'i tshe gźon-nu byaṅ-chub-sems-dpa' sems-dpa'-chen-po yaṅ-dag-pa ji-lta-ba bzin-du chos thams-cad-kyi dṅos-po-med-pa'i ṅo-bo-ñid-kyi ye-śes-la mkhas-pa źes bya'o //

// gźon-nu byaṅ-chub-sems-dpa' sems-dpa'-chen-po chos thams-cad-kyi dṅos-po-med-pa'i ṅo-bo-ñid-kyi ye-śes-la mkhas-pa de-ni gzugs daṅ sgra daṅ dri daṅ reg-bya daṅ chos thams-cad-la 'dod-chags-par mi-byed / źe-sdaṅ-bar mi-byed/gti-mug-par mi-byed-do//de ci'i phyir źe-na / 'di-ltar des chos de yaṅ-dag-par rjes-su-mi-mthoṅ-źiṅ/chos de mi-dmigs-te //

// gaṅ 'dod-chags-pa daṅ gaṅ-la 'dod-chags-pa daṅ gaṅ-gis 'dod-chags-pa daṅ gaṅ źe-sdaṅ-ba daṅ gaṅ-la źe-sdaṅ-ba daṅ gaṅ-gis źe-sdan-ba daṅ gaṅ gti-mug-pa daṅ gaṅ-la gti-mug-pa daṅ gaṅ-gis gti-mug-par -'gyur-ba'i chos de des yaṅ-dag-par-rjes-su-mi-mthoṅ-źin mi-dmigs-so // chos de yaṅ-dag-par-rjes-su mi-mthoṅ-źiṅ mi [18])-dmigs-na khams-gsum thams-cad-la ma-

---

[1]) A śabda. [2]) A *om*. [3]) C rakṛte. [4]) C dṛṣyate. [5]) A *ad* yatra vā duṣyeta yena. [6]) C mute. [7]) A dharme, B dhamam, C dharman. [8]) B dhamam. [9]) C °labhyate. [10]) B yata. [11]) A tayo. [12]) C draṣyeta. [13]) B duṣyātra. [14]) CD *om*. yena vā duṣyeta. [15]) B *om*. [16]) A *om*. sa taṃ dharmaṃ. [17]) anadhyav° c. T., Mss. adhyavasito. [18]) N ma.

cânuttarāṃ samyaksaṃbodhim abhisaṃbudhyate. tatredam ucyate:

chags-par-'gyur-te myur-du tiṅ ṅe-'dzin 'di 'thob-bo // myur-du bla-na-med-pa yaṅ-dag par-rdzogs-pa'i byaṅ-chub kyaṅ mṅon-par-rdzogs-par 'tshaṅ-rgya'o // de-la 'di-skad ces bya-ste //

5) abhāvāḥ sarvadharmā / animittā alakṣaṇā / anutpannā 'niruddhāś ca / evaṃ dharmān vijānatha. /

// chos-rnams thams-cad dṅos-po-med-pa-ste/thams-cad mtshan-ma-med-ciṅ mtshan-ñid-med / skyes-pa-med-ciṅ 'gags-pa-med-par yaṅ / de-ltar chos-rnams śin-tu-rig-par-gyis //

6) abhāvā 'nakṣarāḥ sarve [1]) / śūnyāḥ śāntâdinirmalāḥ [2]) / ya evaṃ jānatī dharmān [3]) / kumārā buddha socyate. /

// thams-cad dṅos-po-med-ciṅ yi-ge-med / stoṅ-pa źi-ba gzod-nas-dri-ma-med / de-ltar chos-rnams gaṅ-gis śes-pa-ni / gźon-nu de-ni saṅs-rgyas źes kyaṅ brjod //

7) tasmāddhi yo icchi vipañcitām [4]) imāṃ [9]) / svabhāvasamatāṃ [5]) sugatāna mātāṃ [6]) sa bhāvayatu [7]) sarvi abhāvadharmāṃ [8]) / pratilapsyatîmāṃ [9]) jananīṃ [10]) jinānāṃ. /

// de-phyir raṅ-bźin mñam-ñid rnam [18])-spros-pa / ṅo-bo-ñid-gyis [19]) chos kun raṅ-bźin-med / bde-bar-gśegs-pa'i yum 'di su 'dod-pa / rgyal-ba-rnams-kyi yum 'di 'thob-par 'gyur. //

8) tad anenâpi te kumāra paryāyeṇaivaṃ veditavyaṃ. bhūtapūrvaṃ kumārâtite 'dhvany asaṃkhyeyaiḥ kalpair [11]) asaṃkhyeyatarair [12]) vipulair [13]) aprameyair [14]) acintyair [15]) aparimāṇair [16]) yadâsīt [17]) tena kālena tena samayena Abhāvasamudgato nāma tathāgato 'rhan samyaksambuddho

// gźon-nu de-lta-bas-na rnam-graṅs 'dis kyaṅ 'di-ltar rig-par bya-ste / gźon-nu sṅon-byuṅ-ba 'das-pa'i dus-na bskal-pa graṅs-med-pa bas kyaṅ chos graṅs-med-pa / rgya-che-ba / gźal-du-med-pa / bsam-gyis-mi-khyab-pa/ tshad-med-par gyur-pa de'i tshe de'i dus-na de-bźin-gśegs-pa /

---

[1]) D sarva. [2]) A °nirmita, B nirmittaḥ, D śādinirmitāḥ. [3]) A dharmāna, C dharmā. [4]) C vipacitām. [5]) C samato. [6]) ABD mātā. [7]) A sa bhāvayāt tu, BD sa bhāvayātu, C svabhāvāyatu. [8]) A °dharmāṇa. [9]) C imā. [10]) B jananām, C jananī. [11]) C asakhyeyai kalpai [12]) B °tara. [13]) C *om.* [14]) C °meye. [15]) B antyair, C acintye. [16]) C °māne. [17]) C yadāśī. [18]) N rnams. [19]) Mss. kyis.

loka udapādi[1]) vidyācaraṇasampannaḥ sugato lokavid anuttaraḥ puruṣadamyasārathiḥ śāstā devānāṃ ca manuṣyānāṃ ca buddho bhagavāṃs.

9) tat kim manyase kumāra kena[2]) kāraṇena sa tathāgato 'bhāvasamudgata ity ucyate? sa khalu punaḥ kumāra[3]) tathāgato jātamātra evopary antarīkṣe saptatālamātram atyudgamya[4]) sapta padāni prakramitvā imām evaṃrūpāṃ[5]) vācam abhāṣata[6]): abhāvasamudgatāḥ sarvadharmā abhāvasamudgatāḥ sarvadharmā iti. tena ca kumāra śabdena trisāhasramahāsāhasro lokadhātuḥ svareṇâbhivijñapto[7]) 'bhūt.

10) tatra bhaumān devān upādāya yāvad brahmalokaṃ paramparayā śabdam udīrayāmāsur ghoṣam anuśrāvayāmāsuḥ[8]): Abhāvasamudgato vatâyaṃ tathāgato bhaviṣyati yo jātamātra evopary antarīkṣe saptatālamātram atyudgamya sapta padāni prakramitvā abhāvaśabdam udīrayatîti hy Abhāvasamudgato 'bhāvasa-

dgra - bcom - pa / yaṅ - dag - par-rdzogs-pa'i saṅs-rgyas / rig-pa-daṅ-źabs-su-ldan - pa / bde - bar-gśegs-pa / 'jig-rten-mkhyen-pa / skyes-bu-'dul-ba'i kha-lo-sgyur-ba / bla-na-med-pa / lha daṅ mi-rnams-kyi ston-pa / saṅs-rgyas / bcom-ldan -'das / dṅos-po-med-pa-las-byuṅ-ba źes bya-ba 'jig-rten-du byuṅ-ṅo //

// gźon-nu 'di ji-sñam-du sems / ci'i phyir de-bźin-gśegs-pa de dṅos-po-med-pa-las-byuṅ-ba źes bya źe-na / gźon-nu de-bźin-gśegs-pa de skyes-ma-thag-tu steṅ-gi nam-mkha'-la ta-la bdun tsam-du 'phags-nas gom-pa bdun bor-te tshig[9]) 'di-skad gsuṅ-ṅo // chos thams-cad dṅos-po-med-pa-las-byuṅ ṅo // chos thams-cad dṅos-po-med-pa - las - byuṅ - ba'o źes gsuṅs-te / gźon-nu sgra de'i dbyaṅs-kyis stoṅ-gsum-gyi stoṅ-chen-po'i 'jig-rten-gyi khams go-bar byas-so //

// de-nas sa'i lha-nas bzuṅs-te tshaṅs-pa'i 'jig-rten-gyi bar-du sgra bsgrags-śiṅ dbyaṅs-kyis rjes-su-go-bar byas-te / e-ma de-bźin-gśegs-pa 'di skyes-ma-thag-tu steṅ-gi nam-mkha'-la ta-la bdun srid-du 'phags-nas gom-pa bdun bor-te / dṅos-po-med-pa'i sgra 'byin-pa-las-na dṅos-po-med-pa-las-byuṅ-ba źes bya-bar 'gyur-

[1]) C utpādi. [2]) B tena. [3]) C kumāraḥ. [4]) C antyudgamya. [5]) B °rūpā. [6]) B abhāṣadga. [7]) B °vijñako, C vittaptā. [8]) C unuśrāv°. [9]) N chig.

mudgata[1]) iti tasya tathāgatasya nāmadheyam udapādi.

ro // źes mtshan dṅos-po-med-pa-las-byuṅ-ba / dṅos-po-med-pa-las-byuṅ-ba'o źes btags-so //

11) tasya ca Bhagavato bodhiprāptasya sarvavṛkṣapatrebhyaḥ sarvatṛṇagulmauṣadhivanaspatibhyaḥ sarvaśailaśikharebhyaś câbhāvasamudgataśabdo niścarati. yāvatī[2]) ca tatra lokadhātau śabdaprajñaptiḥ sarvataḥ[3]) abhāvasamudgatavijñaptiśabdo[4]) niścarati.

// bcom-ldan-'das de byaṅ-chub thob-pa-na śiṅ thams-cad-kyi lo-ma daṅ rtsba[10]) daṅ śiṅ-gel-pa daṅ nags-tshal thams-cad daṅ ri'i rtse-mo tham-cad-las kyaṅ dṅos-po-med-pa-las-byuṅ-ba'o źes sgra byuṅ-ṅo // 'jig-rten-gyi khams de-na sgrar btags-pa ji-sñed yod-pa thams-cad-las dṅos-po-med-pa-las-byuṅ-ba'o źes rnam-par-rig-par byed-pa'i sgra byuṅ-ṅo //

12) tena ca kumāra kālena tena ca samayena tasya bhagavato Abhāvasamudgatasya tathāgatasya 'rhataḥ samyaksambuddhasya pravacanena Mahākaruṇācintī nāma rājakumāro 'bhūd abhirūpaḥ prāsādiko darśanīyaḥ.

// gźon-nu de'i tsche de'i dus-na bcom-ldan-'das / de-bźin-gśegs-pa / dgra-bcom-pa / yaṅ-dag-par-rdzogs-pa'i saṅs-rgyas / dṅos-po-med-pa-las-byuṅ-ba de'i gsuṅ-rab-la rgyal-bu gźon-nu sñiṅ-rje-chen-po-sems śes bya-ba gzugs-bzaṅ źiṅ mdzes-pa[11]) bltana-sdug-pa[11]) źig byuṅ-ṅo //

13) atha khalu kumāra Mahākaruṇācintī nāma rājakumāro[5]) yena bhagavān Abhāvasamudgatas tathāgato 'rhan[6]) samyaksambuddhas tenopasaṃkramya[7]) tasya[8]) bhagavataḥ pādau śirasâbhivandya taṃ[9]) bhagavan-

// gźon-nu de-nas rgyal-bu-gźon-nu sñiṅ-rje-chen-po-sems de bcom-ldan-'das / de-bźin-gśegs-pa / dgra-bcom-pa / yaṅ-dag-par-rdzogs-pa'i saṅs-rgyas / dṅos-po-med-pa-las-byuṅ-ba ga-la-ba-der soṅ-ste phyin-nas bcom-ldan-

---

1) C bhāṃvaṃsamudg⁰. A *repeats still once* tathāgato bhaviṣyati yo jātamātra *etc...* udīrayatîti hy Abhāvasamudgata, D *om. the second* Abhāvasamudgata. 2) ABC yāvantī. 3) D ⁰ta. 4) A avabhasasamudgatavijñapti⁰, C abhāvasamudgatavijñaptiḥ sarvataḥ abhāvasamudgatavijñaptiśabdo. 5) C ⁰karuṇācitrī rājakumāro. 6) C tathāgato nāma 'rhan. 7) AD upasaṃkrāma upasaṃkramya, C upasaṃkrāntamadupasaṃkramye. 8) A *om.* 9) A *om.* 10) N rtsa-ba. 11) Mss. la.

taṃ triḥ[1]) pradaksiṇīkṛtyaikānte 'sthāt.

14) atha khalu kumāra sa bhagavān Abhāvasamudgatas tathāgato 'rhan samyaksambuddho Mahākaruṇācintino rājakumārasyâdhyāśayaṃ viditvā imaṃ samādhiṃ deśayāmāsa[2]).

15) sa[3]) imaṃ samādhiṃ śrutvā prasīdati sma[4]) prasannacittaś ca keśaśmaśrūṇy avatārya kāṣāyāṇi vastrāṇi[5]) paridhāya samyag eva śraddhayā agārād anagārikāṃ pravrajito 'bhūt. sa[6]) pravrajitaḥ sann imaṃ[7]) samādhim udgṛhītavān[8]) udgṛhya paryavāpya dhārayitvā vācayitvā bhāvanāyogam anuyukto vyahārṣīt[9]).

16) sa tenaiva kuśalamūlena viṃśatiḥ kalpakoṭyo[10]) na jātu[11]) durgativinipātam agamat viṃśatiś ca buddhakoṭīr[12]) ārāgayāmāsa. sarveṣāṃ ca tesāṃ[13]) tathāgatānām antikād imaṃ samādhim aśrauṣīt[14]). śrutvā ca[15]) tebhyo buddhebhyas[16]) tenodgṛhītaḥ paryavāpto dhārito vācitaḥ pravarttito 'raṇābhāvanayā bhāvito

'das-kyi źabs-la mgo-bos phyag-'tshal[17])-te / bcom-ldan-'das-la lan-gsum bskor-ba-byas-nas phyogs gcig-tu 'dug-go //

// de-nas bcom-ldan-'das / de-bźin-gśegs-pa / dgra-bcom-pa / yaṅ-dag-par-rdzogs-pa'i saṅs-rgyas / dṅos-po-med-pa-las-byuṅ-bas rgyal-bu gźon-nu sñiṅ-rje-chen-po-sems-kyi lhag-pa'i-bsam-pa mkhyen-nas tiṅ-ṅe-'dzin 'di bśad-do //

// de tiṅ-ṅe-'dzin 'di thos-nas rab-tu daṅ-ṅo / sems rab-tu-daṅ-bas skra daṅ kha-spu bregs-te gos ṅur-smrig gyon-nas dad-pas khyim-nas khyim-med-par rab-tu-byuṅ-ṅo // de rab-tu-byuṅ-nas tiṅ-ṅe-'dzin 'di bzuṅ-ste / bzuṅ-źiṅ bcaṅs bklags[18]) kun-chub-par-byas-nas sgom-pa'i rnal-'byor-la rjes-su-brtson-par gnas-te //

// de dge-ba'i rtsa-ba des bskal-pa bye-ba-phrag ni-śur nam-yaṅ ṅan-'gro log-par-lhuṅ-bar ma-soṅ-ṅo // saṅs-rgyas bye-ba-phrag ni-śu mñes-par byas-te / de-bźin-gśegs-pa de-dag thams-cad-las kyaṅ tiṅ-ṅe-'dzin 'di mñan-to // saṅs-rgyas de-dag thams-cad-las mñan-nas kyaṅ bzuṅ-ṅo // kun-chub-par-byas-

[1]) C tri. [2]) A *om.* imaṃ samādhiṃ deśayāmāsa. [3]) A *om. the beginning of this § down to* śraddhayā. [4]) B sa, C *om.* [5]) B vasrāṇi. [6]) C *om.* pravrajito 'bhūt sa. [7]) C imāṃ. [8]) C °tan vā. [9]) C anuyukte vyāharṣīt. [10]) C koṭye. [11]) C jātur. [12]) AB °koṭīm, C °kotīs. [13]) C teṣyaṃ. [14]) B aśroṣīt. [15]) B śrutvaiva. [16]) C buddhebhyo bhagavadbhyas. [17]) N btsal. [18]) Mss. blags.

bahulīkṛto bhāvanāyogam anuyuktaś ca vyahārṣīt [1]).

so // bcaṅs-so / bklags[14])-so / bton-to / ñoṅ-moṅs-pa-med-par bsgoms-śiṅ maṅ-du byas-te / bsgom-pa'i rnal-'byor-la rjes-su-brtson-par gnas-so //

17) sa tenaiva pūrvakena kuśalamūlena viṃśatīnāṃ kalpakoṭīnām abhyayenânuttarāṃ[2]) samyaksambodhim abhisambuddho[3]) 'bhūt Suvicintitārtho [4]) nāma tathāgato 'rhan samyaksambuddho loka udapādi vidyācaraṇasampannaḥ[5]) sugato lokavid anuttaraḥ puruṣadamyasārathiḥ śāstā[6]) devānāṃ ca manuṣyānāṃ ca buddho bhagavān.

// de dge-ba'i rtsa-ba des bskal-pa ni-śu 'das-nas de-bźin-gśegs-pa / dgra-bcom-pa / yaṅ-dag-par-rdzogs-pa'i saṅs-rgyas / don-legs-par-bsams-pa źes bya-ba 'jig-rten-du byuṅ-ste //

18) so 'prameyān[7]) asaṃkhyeyān satvān paripācyâparimāṇānāñ[8])ca satvānām[9]) arthaṃ kṛtvā tataḥ paścāj[10]) jyotir ivendhanakṣayāt parinirvṛto 'bhūt.

// des sems-can graṅs-med dpag-tu-med-pa yoṅs-su-smin-par byas / sems[15])-can tshad-med-pa'i don byas-nas de'i 'og-tu śiṅ-zad-pa'i me ltar yoṅs-su-mya-ṅan-las-'das-so //

19) tad anenâpi te kumāra paryāyeṇaivaṃ veditavyaṃ. tathâyaṃ[11]) samādhir bahukāro [12]) bodhisatvānāṃ mahāsatvānām anuttarasya buddhajñānasya paripūraṇāya[13]) saṃvartate.

// gźon-nu de-lta-bas-na rnam-graṅs 'dis kyaṅ 'di-ltar tiṅ-ṅe-'dzin 'di byaṅ-chub-sems-dpa' sems - dpa' - chen - po - rnams - kyi gces-spres[16])-byed-pa-ste / saṅs-rgyas-kyi ye-śes bla-na-med-pa yoṅs-su-rdzogs-par-byed-pa yin-par bya'o //

20) atha khalu Bhagavāṃs tasyāṃ velāyāṃ bhūyasyā mā-

// de-nas yaṅ bcom-ldan-'das-kyis de'i tshe zla'-'od-gźon-nur

---

[1]) B vyahīrṣīt, C vyāhāraṣīt. [2]) B abhyena⁰. [3]) BC ⁰buddhā. [4]) AD avicinti⁰, B asauvacintitārthau. [5]) ABD *om. from* vidyācaraṇa... *down to the end of the §*. [6]) C śāntā. [7]) C śāprameyām. [8]) A pratipācya⁰. [9]) ABD *ad.* ca. [10]) C pata. [11]) ACD yathāyaṃ. [12]) D ⁰kăro. [13]) A pūraṇāya. [14]) P blags. [15]) P sams. [16]) Mss. sbras.

trayā[1]) etam[2]) eva[3]) pūrvayogaparivarttaṃ[4]) Candraprabhasya Kumārabhūtasya vistareṇa gāthābhigītena samprakāśayati sma.

21) smarāmy ahaṃ pūrvam atītam-adhvanī / acintiye kalpi[5]) narāṇam uttamaḥ / utpannu lokārthakaro[6]) maharṣi[7]) / nāmnā hi so[8]) 'bhāvasamudgato 'bhūt. /

22) sa jātamātro gagane sthihitvā / sarvāṇa[9]) dharmāṇa[10]) abhāvu[11]) deśayī[12]) / tadânurūpaṃ kṛtu[13]) nāmadheyaṃ / śabdena sarvaṃ[14]) trisahasra vijñapī[15]) /

23) devâpi sarve pramumocu[16]) śabdaṃ / abhāvu nāmneti[17]) jino bhaviṣyati / yo jātamātraḥ[18]) pada sapta prakramann / abhāvu[19]) dharmāṇa bravīti nāyakaḥ[20]). /

24) buddho yadā bheṣyati dharmarājaḥ[21]) / sarvāṇa[9]) dharmāṇa prakāśako muniḥ/tṛṇavṛkṣagulmauṣadhiśailaparvate[22])/ abhāvadharmāṇa ravo bhaviṣyati. /

25) yāvanti śabdās[23]) tahi lokadhātau / sarve[24])hy abhāvā[25])

gyur-pa-la sṅon-byuṅ-ba'i le'u 'di-ñid rgyas-par tshigs-su bcad-pa'i dbyaṅs-kyis rgya-cher yaṅ-dag-par-rab-tu-bstan-to //

// sṅon 'das dus-kyi bskal-pa bsam-yas-na / mi-yi gtso-bo byuṅ-ba ṅas dran-te /draṅ-sroṅ-chen-po gziṅs-kyi[26]) don mdzad-pa / de miṅ dṅos-po-med-las-byuṅ źes bya //

// skyes-ma-thag-tu mkha'-la rab-tu[27])-gnas / chos-rnams thams-cad dṅos-po-med-par bstan / de tshe de daṅ mthun[28])-par mtshan btags-te / sgras ni 'jig-rten kun-tu[29]) grags-par byas //

// lha-rnams thams-cad rab-tu sgra 'byin-pa / dṅos-po-med ces bya-ba'i rgyal-bar 'gyur / skyes-ma-thag-tu gom-pa bdun bor-te / rgyal-bas chos-rnams dṅos-po-med-par bśad //

// thub-pa chos-rnams thams-cad ston-pa-yi / saṅs-rgyas chos-kyi rgyal-por nam 'gyur tshe / rtsba[30])-śiṅ-gel-pa ri daṅ brag-rnams-las / chos-rnams dṅos-po-med ces sgra yaṅ byuṅ //

// 'jig-rten de-na ji-sñed sgra yod-pa / thams-cad dṅos-med ci-

---

1) C mātrayă. 2) C tam. 3) B evaṃ. 4) C *om.* pūrva°. 5) BD acintiya kalpa. 6) C lokārthaṅkaro. 7) C marhaṣīta. 8) C nāmnā hy asau, Pr. nāmena so. 9) A sarveṣa. 10) Pr. °ṇām. 11) Pr. abhāva. 12) Pr. °yĭ. 13) C kṛtun, Pr. kṛta 14) BD °vaḥ, Pr. °va. 15) DPr. vijñayī. 16) BC °moca. 17) C abhāva nāmno ti, Pr. abhāvanāmeti. 18) BCD °tro. 19) Pr. °va. 20) Pr. samaṃ prakāśayī. 21) BD °rājā. 22) Pr. tṛṇagulmavṛkṣa°. 23) A sarvās. 24) BC sarva. 25) BC °vă. 26) Mss. kyis. 27) Mss. 'du. 28) P 'thun. 29) Mss. du. 30) Mss. rtsa.

na hi kaści[1]) bhāvaḥ / tāvantu kho tasya[2]) tathāgatasya / svaru[3]) niścarī lokavināyakasya. /

26) tasmiṃś ca kāle abhu rājaputro / Karuṇāvicintī sada nāmadheyo / abhirūpu[4]) prāsādiku[5]) darśanīyo / upāgamī[6]) tasya jinasya antikam. /

27) vanditva pādau munipuṅgavasya[7]) / pradakṣiṇaṃ kṛtya[8]) ca gauraveṇa / prasannacitto niṣasāda tatra / śravaṇāya dharmaṃ virajam anuttaraṃ[9]). /

28) so ca jjino[10]) āśayu[11]) jñātva dhīro / prakāśayāmāsa samādhim etaṃ / śrutvā ca so imu virajaṃ samādhiṃ / laghu pravrajī jinavaraśāsanasmin[12]). /

29) sa pravrajitvāna imaṃ samādhiṃ / dhāritva vācitva paryāpuṇitvā / kalpāna koṭyaḥ paripūrṇa viṃśati[13]) / na jātu jagme[14]) vinipātabhūmiṃ[15]). /

30) sa tena caiva kuśalena[16]) karmaṇā / ārāgayī viṃśati buddhakoṭyaḥ[17]) / teṣāṃ ca sarveṣa[18]) jināna antike[19]) / imaṃ varaṃ śāntaṃ samādhiṃ bhāvayī. /

'aṅ med.pa źes / de-lta-bur ni 'jig-rten-'dren-pa-yi sgra-dbyaṅs rnam-pa-śin-tu[20])-byuṅ-bar-gyur //

// de'i dus-na rgyal-po'i bu skyes-pa / miṅ ni rtag-tu sñiṅ-rje-sems śes[20]) bya / śin-tu[21])-gzugs bzaṅ blta-na-sdug-pa źig / rgyal-ba de-yi druṅ-du ñer-'oṅs-te //

// thub-pa khyu-mchog źabs-la phyag-'tsal-nas / ri-mor bcas-pas bskor-bar byas-nas ni / rdul-bral bla-na-med-pa'i chos mñan phyir / rab-tu-daṅ-ba'i sems-kyis der 'dug-go //

// rgyal-ba[22]) dpa'-bo des ni bsam mkhyen-nas / tiṅ-'dzin 'di ni rab-tu-bśad-pa mdzad[23]) des ni rdul-bral tiṅ-'dzin 'di thos-nas / rgyal-mchog bstan-la myur-bar rab-tu-byuṅ //

// rab-tu de byuṅ tiṅ-'dzin 'di yaṅ ni / bzuṅ-źiṅ bklags-te yoṅs-su-chub-byas-pas / bskal-pa bye-ba ñi-śu tshaṅ-bar ni / log-par-lhuṅ-ba'i sar yaṅ yod ma-soṅ //

// de ni dge-bar byas-pa'i las de-yis / saṅs-rgyas bye-phrag ñi-śu mñes-par byas / rgyal-ba de-dag kun-gyi druṅ-du yaṅ / tiṅ-'dzin źi mchog 'di ni goms-par byas //

---

1) BC kaś ca. 2) ABD tāvanty ato, C tāvātta khyāt tasya, Pr. (278_{11}) tāvanti kho tasya. 3) Pr. (278_{12}) ravu. 4) B abhipūpu, CD °rūpa. 5) C prāsādika. 6) C upāgamī. 7) B anipuṅgav°, C munipudgalasya. 8) BC kṛtvā. 9) B anuraṃ. 10) CD ca jino. 11) D aśaya, 12) A śāsanesmin. 13) BD viṃśatir. 14) ABD jagmur, C garccha (?). 15) C vinipābhūmiṃ. 16) B kulena. 17) A °koṭayaḥ, B °koṭyeḥ. 18) C sarveṣā. 19) A atikād, D antika. 20) N źes. 21) Mss. du. 22) P po. 23) Mss. mdzod.

31) sa paścakāle abhu buddha loke / Suvicintitārtho sada nāmadheyo / kṛtvā ca arthaṃ bahuprāṇakoṭināṃ / sa paścakālasmi [1]) śikhîva nirvṛtaḥ[2]). /

// de-phyis 'jig-rten-du yaṅ saṅs-rgyas gyur / miṅ ni don-legs-bsams-śes rtag-tu brjod / sems-can bye-ba maṅ-po'i don byas-nas / phyi-ma'i dus-la me bźin mya-ṅan-'das //

iti Abhāva[3])samudgataparivartto nāmo 'ṣṭhamaḥ.

// dṅos-po-med-pa-las-byuṅ-ba'i le'u-ste brgyad-pa'o //

XIX.

1) tatra khalu Bhagavān punar api Candraprabhaṃ Kumārabhūtam āmantrayate sma. tasmāt tarhi kumāra bodhisatvena mahāsatvenemāni[4]) sarvadharmasvabhāvasamatāvipañcitāt[5]) samādher[6]) acintyāny[7]) aprameyāni[8]) guṇānuśaṃsanirhārapadāni[9]) śrūtvā nottrasitukāmena na santrasitukāmena[10]) na santrāsam āpattukāmena[11]) acintyabuddhadharmanirdeśakuśalena [12]) bhavitavyaṃ.

// de-nas yaṅ bcom-ldan-'das-kyis zla'-'od-gźon-nur-gyur-pa-la bka'-stsal-pa gźon-nu de-lta-bas-na byaṅ-chub-sems-dpa' sems-dpa'-chen-po chos thams-cad-kyi raṅ-bźin-mñam-pa-ñid-rnam-par-spros-pa'i tiṅ-ṅe-'dzin-las yon-tan-gyi phan-yon bsam-gyis-mi-khyab-ciṅ dpag-tu-med-pa thos-nas mi-skrag-par 'dod-pa daṅ mi-dṅaṅ-bar 'dod-pa daṅ dṅaṅ-bar mi-'gyur-bar 'dod-pas saṅs-rgyas-kyi chos bsam-gyis-mi-khyab-pa bstan-pa-la mkhas-par bya'o //

2) acintyabuddhadharmādhimuktikena [13]) bhavitavyaṃ, acin-

// saṅs-rgyas-kyi chos bsam-gyis-mi-khyab-pa-la mos-par

---

[1]) BD °lesmi. [2]) C nivṛtiḥ. [3]) A avabhāsa°. [4]) AD °mān. [5]) Mss. °tāyāḥ [6]) B °dhir. [7]) ABC acintyān, C acintitān. [8]) Mss. °yāṃ. [9]) BC °padā, AD °padān. [10]) A samsittuk°. [11]) BC santrasapatuk°. [12]) B °nirdeṣyati vācayiṣyati paryavāpsyati pravarttayiṣyati *and continues as at § 4 down to the end and at the beginning of § 5 down to* Candraprabhasya Kumārabhūtasya. *Then follows* sakusalena bhavitavyaṃ *and afterwards regularly § 2.* [13]) A *omits the whole beginning down to* paryeṣaṇakuśalena bhavitavyaṃ, C antyacibuddhadharmavimuktikena, D °dharmâdhikārâdhimuktena.

tyabuddhadharmaparipṛcchākuśalena bhavitavyaṃ, acintyabuddhadharmaparyeṣaṇakuśalena bhavitavyaṃ, acintyāṃś ca buddhadharmān śrutvā nottrasitavyaṃ na santrasitavyaṃ na santrāsam āpattavyaṃ.

bya'o / saṅs-rgyas-kyi chos bsam-gyis-mi-khyab-pa yoṅs-su-'dri[8])-ba-la mkhas-par bya'o / saṅs-rgyas-kyi chos bsam-gyis-mi-khyab-pa yoṅs-su-btsal-ba-la mkhas-par bya'o / saṅs-rgyas-kyi chos bsam-gyis-mi-khyab-pa thos-nas mi-skrag mi-dṅaṅ dṅaṅ-bar mi-'gyur-bar bya'o //

3) evam ukte Candraprabhaḥ Kumarabhūto yena Bhagavāṃs tenâñjaliṃ praṇamya Bhagavantam etad avocat: yathā kathaṃ punar Bhagavan bodhisatvo mahāsatvo 'cintyabuddhadharmanirdeśakuśalo bhavati, acintyabuddhadharmādhimuktaś câcintyabuddhadharmaparipṛcchākuśalaś câcintyabuddhadharmaparyesaṇakuśalaś[1]) ca bhavati[2]), acintyāṃś ca buddhadharmān śrutvā nottrasyati[3]) na santrasyati[4]) na santrāsam āpadyate.

// de-skad ces bka'-stsal-pa daṅ / zla'-'od-gźon-nur-gyur-pas bcom-ldan-'das ga-la-ba-der logs-su thal-mo sbyar-ba btud-te bcom-ldan-'das-la 'di-skad ces gsol-to // bcom-ldan-'das 'di ji-lta-bur-na byaṅ-chub-sems-dpa' sems-dpa'-chen-po saṅs-rgyas-kyi chos bsam-gyis-mi-khyab-pa bstan-pa-la mkhas-pa lags / saṅs-rgyas-kyi chos bsam-gyis-mi-khyab-pa-la mos-pa daṅ saṅs-rgyas-kyi chos bsam-gyis-mi-khyab-pa yoṅs-su-'dri-ba-la mkhas-pa daṅ saṅs-rgyas-kyi chos bsam-gyis-mi-khyab-pa thos-nas[9]) mi-skrag mi-dṅaṅ dṅaṅ-bar-mi-'gyur-pa lags //

4) evam ukte[5]) Bhagavān Candraprabhaṃ Kumārabhūtam etad avocat: yaḥ kumāra bodhisatvo mahāsatva imaṃ sarvadharmasvabhāvasamatāvipañcitaṃ[6]) samādhiṃ śroṣyati śrutvā codgrahīṣyati dhārayiṣyati[7]) vācayiṣyati

// de-skad ces gsol-pa daṅ bcom-ldan-'das-kyis zla'-'od-gźon-nur-gyur-pa-la 'di-skad ces bka'-stsal-to / gźon-nu byaṅ-chub-sems-dpa' sems-dpa'-chen-po gaṅ chos thams-cad-kyi raṅ-bźin-mñam-pa-ñid-rnam-par-spros-pa'i

---

1) B caḥ acint⁰. 2) BC bhaviṣyati. 3) B nottasyati. 4) B santrati. 5) C mukta. 6) C *om.* ⁰samatā⁰. 7) B dhārayiṣya nirdiṣyamāneṣu *and omits the rest of his §, which was inserted above, see p. 40, footnote 3.* 8) Mss. dri. 9) N na.

paryavāpsyati pravarttayiṣyati araṇabhāvanayā bhāvayiṣyati [1]) bahulīkariṣyati parebhyaś ca vistareṇa samprakāśayiṣyati, sa kumāra bodhisatvo mahāsatvo 'cintyabuddhadharmanirdeśakuśalo bhaviṣyati, acintyabuddhadharmādhimuktaś ca, acintyabud, dhadharmaparipṛcchākuśalaś ca-ac intyabuddhadharmaparyeṣeṇa kuśalaś ca bhaviṣyati, acintyāmś ca buddhadharmān śrutvā nottrasiṣyati na santrasiṣyati[2]) na santrāsam āpatsyate.

5) asmiṃ[3]) khalu punaḥ sarvadharmasvabhāvasamatāvipañcitāt samādher aprameyaguṇānuśaṃsanirhārapadeṣu Bhagavatā Candraprabhasya Kumārabhūtasya nirdiśyamāṇeṣu[4]) atha khalu Candraprabhaḥ Kumārabhūta imāni sarva dharma svabhāva samatāvipañcitāt[5]) samadher aprameyaguṇānuśaṃsanirhārapadāny acintyāni[6]) Bhagavataḥ śrutvā tasmin samaye Candraprabhaḥ Kumārabhūta imaṃ sarvadharmasvabhā-

tiṅ-ṅe-'dzin 'di ñan-żiṅ[7]) thos-nas kyaṅ 'dzin-pa daṅ / kun-chub-par-byed-pa daṅ / 'chaṅ[8])-ba daṅ klog-pa daṅ / rab-tu-'don-pa daṅ ñon-moṅs-pa-med-par bsgom-pas bsgom[9])-par byed-pa daṅ / maṅ-du-byed-pa daṅ / gźan-la yaṅ rgya-cher yaṅ-dag-par-rab-tu-ston-na gźon-nu byaṅ-chub-sems-dpa' sems-dpa'-chen-po de saṅs-rgyas-kyi chos bsam-gyis-mi-khyab-pa bstan-pa-la mkhas-par 'gyur-ro // saṅs-rgyas-kyi chos bsam-gyis-mi-khyab-pa-la mos-pa daṅ saṅs-rgyas-kyi chos bsam-gyis-mi-khyab-pa yoṅs-su-'dri-ba-la mkhas-pa daṅ saṅs-rgyas-kyi chos bsam-gyis-mi-khyab-pa thos-nas mi-skra mi-dṅaṅ dṅaṅ-bar-mi-'gyur-ro //

// yaṅ chos thams-cad-kyi raṅ-bźin mñam-pa-ñid rnam-par-spros-pa'i tiṅ-ṅe-'dzin-las yon-tan-gyi phan-yon bsgrub-pa'i tshig 'di bcom-ldan-'das-kyis zla'-'od-gźon-nur-gyur-pa-la- ṅes-par-bstan-pa-na / zla'-'od-gźon-nur-gyur-pas chos thams-cad-kyi raṅ-bźin mñam-pa-ñid rnam-par-spros-pa'i tiṅ-ṅe-'dzin-las yon-tan-gyi phan-yon bsgrub-pa'i tshig dpag-tu-med-pa bsam-gyis-mi-khyab-pa bcom-ldan-'das-las thos-nas de'i

---

[1]) C bhavayitiṣyati. [2]) C nottrasyati na santrasyati *(and so* B *in the passage inserted above).* [3]) B *omits the beginning of this § down to* nirdiśyamāṇeṣu, *see p. 39 the f. note 7.* [4]) C nirdeṣyamāṇeṣu. [5]) BC °tāṃ. [6]) BC acintyāṃ. [7]) Mss. ciṅ. [8]) P 'tshaṅ, [9]) N sgom.

vasamatāvipañcitasamādhirājaṃ[1]) pratilabdhavān[2]).

tshe zla'-'od-gźon-nur-gyur-pas chos thams-cad-kyi raṅ-bźin mñam-pa-ñid rnam-par-spros-pa'i tiṅ-ṅe-'dzin-gyi rgyal-po 'di rab-tu-thob-bo //

6) aprameyāsaṃkhyeyāś ca bodhisatvā mahāsatvā mahābhijñānasya[3]) lābhino 'bhūvan[4]), aprameyāṇāṃ ca satvānāṃ[5]) mahākaruṇāvatārābhimukhāni cittāny utpannāni[6]), ayaṃ ca trisāhasramahāsāhasro lokadhātuḥ ṣaḍvikāraṃ[7]) kampitaḥ[8]) prakampitaḥ[9]) saṃprakampitaḥ[10]), calitaḥ pracalitaḥ saṃpracalitaḥ, vedhitaḥ pravedhitaḥ saṃpravedhitaḥ, kṣubhitaḥ prakṣubhitaḥ saṃprakṣubhitaḥ[11]) raṇitaḥ praraṇitaḥ saṃpraraṇitaḥ garjitaḥ pragarjitaḥ saṃpragarjitaḥ.

// byaṅ-chub-sems-dpa' sems dpa'-chen-po graṅs-med dpag-tu-med-pa yaṅ mṅon-par-śes-pa chen-po thob-par gyur-to // sems-can dpag-tu-med-pa yaṅ sñiṅ-rje-chen-por 'jug-pa-la mṅon-du-phyogs-pa'i sems skyes-so // stoṅ-gsum-gyi stoṅ chen-po'i 'jig-rten-gyi khams 'di yaṅ rnam-pa drug-tu gyos rab-tu-gyos kun-tu-rab-tu-gyos / 'gul rab-tu-'gul kun-tu-rab-tu-'gul / ldeg[14]) rab-tu-ldeg[14]) kun-tu-rab-tu-ldeg[14]) / 'khrugs rab-tu-'khrugs kun-tu-rab-tu-'khrugs / chem-chem rab-tu-chem-chem kun-tu-rab-tu-chem-chem / 'ur-'ur rab-tu-'ur-'ur kun-tu-rab-tu-'ur-'ur //

7) pūrvā dig avanamati paścimā dig unnamati, paścimā dig avanamati pūrvā dig unnamati, uttarā dig avanamati dakṣiṇā dig unnamati, dakṣiṇā dig avanamati[12]) uttarā dig unnamati, antād avanamati madhyād unnamati, madhyād avanamati antād unnamati.

// śar-phyogs dma'-na nub-phyogs mtho / nub-phyogs dma'-na śar-phyogs mtho / byaṅ-phyogs dma'-na lho-phyogs mtho / lho-phyogs dma'-na byaṅ-phyogs mtho / mtha' dma'-na dbus mtho / dbus dma'-na mtha' mtho źiṅ //

8) aprameyasya[13]) câvabhāsasya loke prādurbhāvo 'bhūt,

// snaṅ-ba dpag-tu-med-pa yaṅ 'jig-rten-du byuṅ / lha'i spos-kyi

---

[1]) B °raja. [2]) B pralabdhavān. [3]) C *om.* mahā. [4]) B bhuvanaṃ, C 'bhuvana. [5]) C satvānyaṃ. [6]) B upannāni. [7]) ABD °ra. [8]) B prakampitaḥ. [9]) C prakampika, D kamprapita. [10]) B *om.* [11]) B pakṣubhitaḥ sampakṣubhitaḥ. [12]) A *om.* dakṣiṇā dig avanamat'. [13]) A apramāṇasya. [14]) P lhag.

mahac ca divyagandhavarṣam abhiprāvarṣat, yāvantaś ca devā[1]) devaputrāś[2]) ca sannipatitāḥ sanniṣaṇṇāś[3]) ca dharmaśravaṇāya te upary antarīkṣe 'bhyudgamyemāni[4]) sarvadharmasvabhāvasamatāvipañcitāt[5]) samādher aprameyāni[6]) guṇānuśaṃsanirhārapadāni[7]) śrutvā te sarve devā devaputrāś ca tuṣṭā udagrā āttamanaskāḥ[8]) pramuditāḥ prītisaumanasyajātāḥ[9]) hāhākāra kilikilā [10]) prakṣveḍitanirnādanirghoṣāṇy[11]) akārṣuḥ.

char chen-po yaṅ mṅon-par-babpo // lha daṅ lha'i bu ji-sñed chos mñan-pa'i phyir 'dus-te lhags-pa de-dag nam-mkha'-la mṅon-par-'phags-nas chos thams-cad-kyi raṅ-bźin mñam-pa-ñid rnam-par-spros-pa'i tiṅ-ṅe-'dzin-las yon-tan-gyi phan-yon-gyi tshig dpag-tu-med-pa 'di-dag thos-nas lha daṅ lha'i-bu de-dag thams-cad dga' mgu yid [20])-raṅs-te / rab-tu-dga'ba daṅ tshim-pa daṅ yid-bde-ba-skyes-na a-la-la źes ga-źa sgrogs-pa'i sgra byed-do //

9) mahāntaṃ ca nānāvidhadivyapuṣpavarṣam avasṛjanti[12])sma, divyāni cânekāni[13]) tūryakoṭiniyutaśatasahasrāṇi parāhananti[14])sma evaṃ caikodāhārasvareṇa vāco bhāṣante sma: aho sulabdhā asmākaṃ lābhāḥ, yair asmābhir imāni aprameyaguṇānuśaṃsanirhārapadāni Bhagavato 'ntikācchrutāni.

// lha'i me-tog rnam-pa-sna-tshogs-kyi me-tog-gi char chen-po 'bebs-so // lha'i sil-sñan bye-ba khrag-khrig brgya-stoṅ du-ma yaṅ rab-tu-rduṅ-ṅo // brjod-pa gcig-pa'i dbyaṅs[21])-kyis tshig 'di-skad ces 'dzer-to // a-la-la bdag-cag-gis ni rñed-pa legs-par-rñed-do 'di-ltar bdag-cag-gis bcom-ldan-'das-las yon-tan-gyi phan-yon bsgrub-pa'i tshig dpag-tu-med-pa 'di-dag thos-nas //

10) te vayam Bhagavan sarve sahitāḥ[15]) samagrā[16]) yathâryaś[17]) Candraprabho bodhisatvo mahāsatvaḥ sarvadharmasvabhāvasamatāvipañcitasya samādher[18]) lābhī[19]) tathā vayam api Bhagavan

bcom-ldan-'das bdag-cag thams-cad kyaṅ gcig-car[22]) mthun[23])-par byaṅ-chub-sems-dpa' sems-dpa'-chen-po zla-'od-gźon-nur-gyur-pas ji-ltar chos thams-cad-kyi raṅ-bźin-mñam-pa-ñid rnam-

---

1) BC deva. 2) BC ⁰tras. 3) B saniṣarṇāś, C sanniṣarṇāś. 4) Mss. imāṃ 5) B tā, C tāṃ. 6) Mss. aprameyāṃ, 7) ABD ⁰padāṃ; C nirhāpadāṃ. 8) BC ātmanaskāḥ. 9) BC prītir somanasyajātā. 10) A kilakilā. 11) BC ⁰prakṣetrita⁰ (?), C ⁰ninada⁰. 12) BC ⁰jati. 13) BC *ad.* ca. 14) C ⁰nati. 15) A samāhitāḥ. 16) A samayā. 17) B yathāyaś. 18) BC samādhe. 19) C labhīta. 20) N yi. 21) P dbyaṅ N bbyaṅs. 22) P char. 23) P 'thun.

sarva[1]) evaṃvidhasyaiva sarvadharmasvabhāvasamatāvipañcitasya samādher[2]) lābhino bhavema iti.

par-spros-pa'i tiṅ-ṅe-'dzin 'di thob-pa de-bźin-du bcom-ldan-'das bdag-cag thams-cad-kyis kyaṅ chos thams-cad-kyi[13]) raṅ-bźin-mñam-pa-ñid-rnam-par-spros-pa'i tiṅ-ṅe-'dzin 'di thob-par bgyi'o //

11) tena khalu punaḥ samayena Gṛdhrakūṭe parvate Bhagavataḥ[3]) sāgaropamāyāṃ parṣadi dharmaṃ deśayataḥ Pañcaśikho[4]) nāma gandharvaputraḥ pañcabhis tūryaśataiḥ sārddhaṃ gaganatalād avatīrya[5]) Bhagavataḥ purataḥ sthito 'bhūd upasthānaparicaryāyai[6]).

// de-nas de'i tshe bya-rgod-kyi phuṅ-po'i ri-la bcom-ldan-'das 'khor-rgya-mtsho'i naṅ-na chos ston-pa-la dri-za'i bu gtsug-phud-lṅa-can źes bya-ba rim-gro daṅ bsñen-bkur-bya-ba'i phyir sil-sñan lṅa-brgya daṅ bcas-te nam-mkha'-las babs-nas bcom-ldan-'das-kyi spyan-sṅar 'dug-go //

12) atha khalu Pañcaśikhasya gandharvaputrasyaitad abhavat: yaṃ nv ahaṃ yathaiva devānān trayastriṃśāṇām Śakrasya ca devānām indrasya Sudharmāyāṃ devasabhāyām upasthānaparicaryāṃ[7]) karomi saṃgītiṃ saṃprayojayāmi[8]), tathaivâdya[9]) devātidevasyâpi[10]) tathāgatasyârhataḥ[11]) samyaksaṃbuddhasya pūjāyai saṃgītiṃ saṃprayojayeyaṃ.

// de-nas dri-za'i bu gtsug-phud-lṅa-can 'di-sñam-du sems-te / bdag-cag-gis sum-cu[14])-rtsa-gsum-pa'i lha-rnams daṅ lha'i dbaṅ-po brgya-byin-gyi lha'i 'dun-sa chos-bzaṅ-na ji-lta-ba bźin-du rim-gro daṅ bsñen-bkur bya'o / glu-dbyaṅs-dag ji-ltar len-pa de-bźin-du deṅ lha'i lha de-bźin-gśegs-pa dgra-bcom-pa yaṅ-dag-par-rdzogs-pa'i śaṅs-rgyas-la yaṅ mchod-pa'i phyir glu-dbyaṅs rab-tu-sbyar-ro //

13) atha khalu Pañcaśikho[4]) gandaharvaputras taiḥ[12]) pañcabhis tūryaśataiḥ sārddham eka-

// de-nas dri-za'i bu gtsug-phud-lṅa-can sil-sñan thogs-pa lṅa-brgya-pa de-dag daṅ sgra

---

1) AC sarve. 2) BC samādhe. 3) B bhavagataḥ. 4) BC °khyo. 5) C vatīrya. 6) A °paricaryā, B bhūyad usthāna°. C *om.* upasthānaparicaryāyai. 7) A *om. the beginning of this § down to* upasthānaparicaryām. 8) C °yojāmi. 9) A tathaivāya. 10) BD devānti°. 11) A tathāgata *and om. the rest of the §.* 12) BC traiḥ. 13) N chos kyi. 14) P bcu.

svarasaṃprayuktair [1] vaiḍūryadaṇḍāṃ[2] vīṇāṃ svayam ādāya Bhagavataḥ purato vādayāmāsa.

gcig-tu sbyar-te / pi-waṅ-gi khog-pa bai-du-rya-las byas-pa-dag kyaṅ thogs-nas bcom-ldan-'das-kyi spyan-sṅar blaṅs-so //

14) atha khalu Bhagavata etad abhūt: yaṃ nv ahaṃ tathārūpam ṛddhyabhisaṃskāram abhisaṃskuryāṃ yathārūpeṇa ṛddhyabhisaṃskāreṇâbhisaṃskṛtena Candraprabhaḥ Kumārabhūto acintyabuddhadharmanidhyaptikauśalyam adhigacchet, sarvadharmasvabhāvasamatāvipañcitāc ca samādher[3] na[4] calet, Pañcaśikhasya gandharvaputrasya tantrīsvaragītisvarakauśalyam [5] upadiśeyam.

// de-nas bcom-ldan-'das 'di sñam-du dgoṅs-te / rdzu-'phrul-mṅon-par-'du-bya-la ji-lta-bu mṅon-par-'dus-byas-pas zla'-'od-gźon-nur-gyur-pa saṅs-rgyas-kyi chos bsam-gyis-mi-khyab-pa ṅes-par-rtogs-pa-la mkhas-pa 'thob-pa daṅ chos thams-cad raṅ-bźin mñam-pa-ñid rnam-par-spros-pa'i tiṅ-ṅe-'dzin-las mi-gyo-ba daṅ / dri-za'i bu gtsug-phud-lṅa-can-la yaṅ rgyud-kyi sgra daṅ glu'i sgra-la mkhas-pa bstan-par 'gyur-ba de-lta-bu'i rdzu-'phrul mṅon-par-'du-bya-ba ṅas bya'o sñam-mo //

15) atha khalu Bhagavāṃs tathārūpam ṛddhyabhisaṃskāram abhisaṃskaroti sma[6], yas tebhyaḥ pañcabhyas tūryaśatebhyaḥ susaṃprayuktebhyaḥ saṃpravāditebhyo yathâcintyārthopasaṃhitaḥ śabdo niścarati dharmatāpratisaṃyuktaḥ, imāś[7] câcintyabuddharmanidhyaptigāthā niścaranti sma[8] buddhānubhavena.

// de-nas bcom-ldan-'das-kyis de-lta-bu'i rdzu-'phrul-mṅon-par-'du-bya-ba mṅon-par-mdzad-de / saṅs-rgyas-kyi mthus sil-sñan lṅa-brgya-po śin-tu [10])-legs-par-sbyar[11])-ba / legs-par-blaṅs-pa de-dag-las bsam-gyis-mi-khyab-pa'i don-daṅ-ldan-pa chos ñid-daṅ-ldan-pa'i sgra byuṅ-ṅo // saṅs rgyas-kyi chos bsam-gyis-mi-khyab-pa ṅes-par-rtogs-pa'i **tshigs-su[12])-bcad-pa 'di-dag kyaṅ** byuṅ-ṅo //

16) ekahi[9]) vālapathe bahu

// **skra-gcig-khyon-la saṅs-**

---

[1]) A *om. the beginning down to* saṃprayuktaiś, B °taiḥ, C °tai. [2]) A °dāṇḍāni. [3]) BC °dhe. [4]) A nā. [5]) AD °gītavara°. [6]) A *om.* [7]) ABC imāṃś. [8]) B samanta, C sama. [9]) AD ekehi, B ekahi *and om. the rest of the stanza.* [10]) P du. [11]) Mss. sbyaṅs. [12]) P tshig bsu.

buddhā / yāttika vālika Gaṅganadīye / kṣetra pi tāttaka[1]) teṣa jinānāṃ / te[2]) ca vilakṣaṇa te[3]) visabhāgāḥ. /

17) pañcagatīgata[4]) vālapathasmi / nairáyikā[5]) pi ca[6]) tiryagatāś ca[7]) / te yamalokika, deva, manuṣyā / nāpi ca saṃkaru no ca upīḍo. /

18) tatra pade sasarāḥ[8]) sasamudrāḥ[9]) / sarvanadī tatha utsataḍāgāḥ / no pi ca saṃkaru no ca upīḍo / evam acintiya [10]) dharma jinānāṃ. /

19) tatra pade pi ca parvat' aneke / Cakravāḍa api Meru Sumeru[11]) / ye[12]) Mucilinda[13]) Mahāmucilinda[13])/Vindhy'atha[14])Gṛdhrakūṭo Himavāṃś ca. /

20) tatra pade nirayāś ca sughorās / tapana pratāpana ānabhiramyāḥ / tatra ca ye niraye[15]) upapannā / vedana te pi dukhām anubhonti./

21) tatra pade pi ca devavimānā / dvādaśa yojana te ramaṇīyā / teṣu[16]) bahū marutāna sahasrā[17]) / divyaratīṣu sukhāny anubhonti. /

rgyas maṅ-po ni / gaṅ-gā'i kluṅ-gi bye-ma ci yod sñed / rgyal-ba de-dag źiṅ yaṅ de-sñed de / de-dag mtshan-ñid-mi-'dra skal [18])-mi-mñam //

// skra-yi khyon-la 'gro-ba lṅa-rnams-te/sems-can-dmyal daṅ dud-'gror-'gro-ba daṅ / gśin-rje'i-'jig-rten lha daṅ mi-rnams źugs / 'dres-pa-med-ciṅ gnod-par-'gyur-ba'aṅ med //

// de-yi gnas-su mtsho daṅ rgya-mtshor bcas / chu-kluṅ de-bźin mtshe'u daṅ lteṅ-ka-rnams / 'dres-pa-med-ciṅ gnod-par-mi-'gyur-te / de-ltar rgyal-ba'i chos ni bsam-mi-khyab //

// de-yi gnas-su ri-bo du-ma ste / khor-yug daṅ ni lhun-po rab-lhun daṅ / btaṅ-zuṅ daṅ ni btaṅ-zuṅ-chen-po daṅ / 'bigs-byed bya-rgod-phuṅ-po gaṅs-kyi-ri //

// gnas der sems-can-dmyal-ba mi-bzaṅ-ba /tsha' daṅ rab-tu-tsha'-ba ñams-mi-dga' / de-na sems-can-dmyal-skyes tshor-ba-yi / sdug-bsṅal de-dag rjes-su-myoṅ-bar byed //

// de-yi gnas-na lha-yi gźal-med-khaṅ/de-dag dpag-tshad bcu-gñis dbyiṅs[19]) dga'-ba / lha-rnams stoṅ-phrag maṅ-po de-dag kyaṅ / lha-yi dga'-ba śin-tu [20])-bde-ba myoṅ //

---

1) A kṣetraṃ tāttaka, D kṣetraṃ tāttika. 2) C ke. 3) C *om.* 4) B *om.* 5) D nairayi. 6) A api *instead of* pi ca. 7) A °tā ca, B °tācca. 8) C śasarāṃ, D śaśasarāḥ. 9) A samudrāḥ. B sasamudrā. 10) A acintiyu. 11) B °ruṃ. 12) *ad.* pi. 13) BC °dra. 14) Mss. Vindhyâtha. 15) A niye. 16) A teṣu ca, B teṣa, C te ca. 17) B °srô, C saharara. 18) P bskal. 19) Mss. dbyaṅs. 20) P du.

22) tatra pade ca[1]) buddhāna utpādo / śāsana lokavidūna jvaleti / tañ ca na paśyati jñānavihīno / yena na śodhita carya[2]) viśuddha.

// de-yi gnas-su saṅs-rgyas-rnams-skye-źiṅ / 'jig-rten-rig-pa'i bstan-pa 'bar-ba-snaṅ / gaṅ-gis rnam-dag - spyod-pa ma-sbyaṅs-pa / ye-śes-bral-ba-dag-gis de mi-mthoṅ //

23) tatra pade pi ca dharmu[3]) niruddho / nirvṛtu nāyaku śrūyati śabdaḥ / tatra pade[4]) pi ca keci[5]) śṛṇontī / tiṣṭhati nāyaku bhāṣati dharmaṃ. /

// de-yi gnas-ñid-na yaṅ chos nub-ciṅ / 'dren-pa mya-ṅan-'das-pa'i sgra yaṅ thos / de-yi gnas-ñid-na yaṅ la-la-yis / 'dren-pa bźugs-te chos kyaṅ ston źes[20]) thos //

24) tatra pade pi ca keṣacid āyur[6]) / varṣa[7]) acintiya varttati saṃjñā / tatra pade pi ca kālu karonti / no ciru[8]) jīvati śrūyati śabdaḥ. /

// de-yi gnas-ñid-na yaṅ la-la-dag / tshe[21])-tshad[22]) lo ni bsam-yas bźugs sñam-'dzin / de-yi gnas-na'aṅ 'chi-ba'i dus byed-ciṅ / riṅ-du mi 'tsho źes ni sgra yaṅ thos //

25) tatra pade pi ca keṣaci saṃjñā / dṛṣṭu[9]) tathāgatu[10]) pūjitu[10]) buddho / toṣitu mānasu saṃjñagraheṇa[11]) / no pi ca pūjitu no ca utpanno. /

// gnas-der la-la 'di-sñam 'du-śes-te / yid-kyi 'du-śes daṅ ni 'dzin-pa-yis / bde-gśegs mthoṅ mchod saṅs-rgyas mñes-byas sñam / skyes-pa-med-ciṅ mchod-pa-byas-pa'aṅ med //

26) svasmi gṛhe supine va manuṣyo / kāmaguṇeṣu ratīm anubhūya / sa pratibuddhu[12]) na paśyati kāmāṃs / tac ca prajānati[13]) so supino[14])ti. /

// mi-dag bdag-gi khyim-na rmi-lam bźin / 'dod-pa'i yon-tan-dag-la dga' myoṅ-nas / phyir sad-nas kyaṅ de-yis 'dod ma-mthoṅ / de-ni rmi-lam yin-par de-yis śes //

27) tatha[15]) dṛṣṭu[16]) śrutaṃ mata[17]) jñātaṃ[18]) / sarvam[19]) idaṃ

// de-bźin mthoṅ thos rig daṅ bye-brag-phyed / 'di-dag thams-

---

[1]) AD tatra ca pade. [2]) BC carye. [3]) B dharma. [4]) BC tatra ca pade. [5]) B kecit. [6]) AC āyu, [7]) BC varṣaṃ. [8]) BC caru. [9]) BC dṛṣṭa. [10]) B °ta. [11]) BC °ṇā. [12]) B °buddhe, C °buddha. [13]) C prajāpati. [14]) D supine. [15]) BC tathā. [16]) BC dṛṣṭa. [17]) B ma. [18]) *I do not change this defective verse, because it is attested in all the Mss., but it seems very probable that there was a regular dodhaka:* yat tatha dṛṣṭu śrutaṃ mata (j)ñātaṃ. [19]) B satvam. [20]) Mss. ces. [21]) P che. [22]) N chad.

vitathe supino[1]) vā / yas tu bhaveta samādhiya lābhī[2]) / so imu jānati dharmasvabhāvaṃ. /

cad mi-bden rmi-lam bźin / gaṅ-gis tiṅ-dzin 'di yaṅ thob - gyur-pa / des ni chos-kyi raṅ-bźin 'di-dag śes //

28) sūsukhitāḥ[3]) sada te nara loke / yeṣa[4]) priyāpriya[5]) nâsti kahiñcit[6]) /ye vanakandarake[7]) 'bhiramanti[8]) / śrāmaṇakaṃ[9]) susukham anubhonti. /

// su-la'aṅ sdug daṅ mi-sdug med-pa-ni / mi de 'jig-rten-na yaṅ bde-skyid rtag / su-dag nags-khrod mṅon-par-dga'-ba-yi / dge-sbyoṅ de ni śin-tu[27])-bde-ba myoṅ //

29) yeṣa[10]) mamâpi tu[11]) nâsti kahiñcit / yeṣa[12]) parigrahu[13]) sarvaśu nâsti / khaḍgasamā vicarant' imu lokam / te[14]) gagane pavane va[15]) vrajanti. //

// su-dag ci-la'aṅ bdag-gir bya-ba-med / yoṅs-su-'dzin-pa rnam-pa-kun-tu spaṅs / bse-ru bźin-du 'jig-rten 'di-na gnas / nam-mkha'-la ni rluṅ daṅ rgyu-ba bźin //

30) bhāvitu[16]) mārgu[17]) pravarttitu[18]) jñānaṃ / śūnyaka dharma nirātmaka[19]) sarve / yena vibhāvita bhont' imi dharmās / tasya bhavet pratibhānam anantaṃ. /

// lam-rnams bsgoms-śiṅ ye-śes rab-tu-źugs / chos-rnams thams-cad stoṅ-pa bdag-med-par / chos-rnams 'di-dag gaṅ-gis rab-bsgoms-pa / de-yi spobs-pa-dag ni mtha'-yas 'gyur //

31) sūsukhitā[20]) vata[21]) te nara loke / yeṣa na sajjati mānasu[22]) loke / vāyusamaṃ sada teṣv iha cittaṃ / no ca priyâpriya vidyati saṃgo. /

// su-dag 'jig-rten-na ni yid chags-med / de-dag sems ni rtag-tu rluṅ daṅ 'dra / sdug daṅ mi-sdug-la yaṅ chags-pa-med / 'jig-rten-na ni mi de śin-tu[27])-skyid[28]) //

32) apriya ye dukhu tehi[23]) nivāso / ye pi priyā dukhu[24]) tehi viyogo[25]) / antu[26]) ubhe api eti jahitvā / te sukhitā nara ye rata dharme. /

// mi-sdug-pa-daṅ-'grogs-pa sdug-bsṅal-te / sdug-pa daṅ yaṅ bral-ba sdug-bsṅal yin / mthar-byas 'di gñis rab-tu-spaṅs-nas ni / mi gaṅ chos-la dga'-ba de-dag skyid[28]) //

---

[1]) BC tapino. [2]) C °bhī. [3]) C susuṣitā. [4]) BCS yeṣu. [5]) B piyāpiy ā C priyāpiya. [6]) B °cat. [7]) S ca nak°. [8]) S °nte. [9]) B śrāvamaṇakaṃ, śrămaṇakaṃ. [10]) S yeṣu. [11]) A mamārpitu. [12]) BCS yeṣu. [13]) BCD °graha. [14]) S *om.* te. [15]) S yathaiva. [16]) BD bhāṣitu. [17]) A mārga. [18]) B °vartatu, C °vantitu [19]) A nirātmaku. [20]) S syuḥ sukhitā. [21]) D va. [22]) BC mānusu, S mānasa. [23]) S dukhitehi. [24]) BC dukha. [25]) B °ga. [26]) S anta. [27]) P du, [28]) P skyed.

33) yo[1]) anunīyati śrutv' imu dharmaṃ[2]) / sa pratihanyati śrutva adharmaṃ[2]) / so madamānahato viparīto / mānavaśena dukham anubhoti. /

// gaṅ-źig chos 'di thos-nas chags-byed-ciṅ / chos ma-yin-pa thos-nas khoṅ-khro byed / ṅa-rgyal-rgyags-pas bcom-pa log-pa de / ṅa-rgyal-dbaṅ-gis sdug-bsṅal rjes-su-myoṅ //

34) ye samatāya[3]) pratiṣṭhita[4]) bhonti / nityam[5]) anunnata[6]) nâvanatāś[7]) ca / ye priyato 'priyataś ca sumuktās / te sada muktamanā viharanti. /

// su-dag mñam-pa-ñid-la rab-gnas-te / rtag-tu kheṅs-pa-med-ciṅ 'dud-pa-med / sdug-daṅ-mi-sdug-pa-las rab-grol-ba / de-dag rtag-tu grol-yid legs-par-gnas //

35) śīle pratiṣṭhita[8]) sūpariśuddhe / dhyāne pratiṣṭhita[8]) nityam acintye / ye vanakandari śānti ramante / teṣa na vidyati vīmati[9]) jātu. /

// tshul-khrims yoṅs-su-dag-par rab-gnas-te / bsam-gtan bsam-mi-khyab-la rtag gnas-śiṅ / su-dag nags[18])-khrod źi-bar dga'-ba ni / de-dag nam-yaṅ yid-gñis yod mi-'gyur //

36) ye ca punar[10]) vitathe[11]) pratipannāḥ / kāmaguṇeṣu[12]) ratāḥ sada bālāḥ / gṛdhra[13]) yathā kuṇapeṣv[14]) adhimuktāḥ / nityavaśānugatā Namuciṣya. /

// mi-bden-pa-la su-dag rab-źugs-śiṅ / byis-pa 'dod-pa'i yon-tan rtag-tu dga' / bya-rgod-dag ni ro-la mos-pa bźin / de-dag rtag-par bdud-kyi dbaṅ-du 'gro //

37) asmiṃ khalu punar gāthābhinirhāre tato[15]) vīṇāśabdān niścaramāṇe[16]) Candraprabhaḥ Kumārabhūto 'cintyeṣu buddhadharmeṣu gambhīranidhyaptinirdeśakauśalyam anuprāptaḥ, Pañcaśikhasya ca gandharvaputrasya ghoṣānugāyāḥ kṣanteḥ pratilambho 'bhūt, aprameyāṇāṃ ca satvānāṃ devamanuṣikāyāḥ[17]) prajāyā anuttarāyāṃ samyaksambo-

// yaṅ pi-waṅ-gi sgra de-las tshigs-su-bcad-pa mṅon-par-bsgrub-pa 'di byuṅ-nas zla-'od-gźon-nur-gyur-pas saṅs-rgyas-kyi chos bsam-gyis-mi-khyab-pa zab-mo ṅes-par-rtogs-pa-la mkhas-pa rjes-su-thob-bo // dri-za'i bu gtsug-phud-lṅa-can yaṅ sgra'i rjes-su-'gro-ba'i bzod-pa thob-par gyur-to // lha daṅ mi-yi skye-dgu sems-can dpag-tu-med-pa bla-na-

---

[1]) D *om.* yo. [2]) Mss. °māṃ. [3]) BC °ye. [4]) A pratiṣṭhitu *and ad.* nityaṃ. [5]) BC nitye, A *om.* nityam *and ins.* na cintya ye vanakandari śantim. [6]) BC anannat a [7]) B vānatās, C nāvanaṃtāś. [8]) A °tu. [9]) A vīmana. [10]) BC vuna. [11]) Mss. °tha. [12]) BC krāma°. [13]) A gṛdhru. [14]) BC °piṣv. [15]) B taṃto. [16]) B °ṇā, C °ṇau [17]) B °kāṃ yāḥ. [18]) Mss. gnas.

dhau cittāny utpannāni, aprameyāṇāṃ ca satvānam arthaḥ[1]) kṛto 'bhūt.

iti acintyabuddhadharmanirdeśaparivartto namonavimśatitamaḥ.

XXII.

1) tatra Bhagavān punar api Candraprabhaṃ Kumārabhūtam āmantrayate sma. tasmāt tarhi kumāra bodhisatvena mahāsatvenemaṃ[2]) samādhim ākāṃkṣatā[3]) kṣipraṃ cânuttarāṃ samyaksaṃbodhim abhisaṃboddhukāmena[4]) kāyajīvite cânadhyavasitena[5])bhavitavyam.

2) tat kasya hetoḥ? kāyajīvitâdhyavasānahetor hi kumāra satvānām akuśalaḥ[6]) karmābhisaṃskāro bhavati.

3) kāyajīvitānadhyavasitānāṃ ca[7]) kumāra bodhisatvānāṃ mahāsatvānāṃ na durlabhā bhavaty[8])anuttarā samyaksambodhiḥ. kim aṅga punar ayaṃ samādhiḥ! tasmāt tarhi kumāra kāyajivitānadhyavasito bhaviṣyamîty evaṃ

med-pa yaṅ-dag-par-rdzogs-pa'i byaṅ-chub-tu sems skyes-so // sems-can dpag-tu-med-pa-rnams-kyi yaṅ don byas-par-gyur-to //

// saṅs-rgyas-kyi chos bsam-gyis-mi-khyab-pa- ṅes-par-bstan-pa'i le'u-ste bcu-dgu-pa'o //

XXII.

// de-nas yaṅ bcom-ldan-'das-kyis zla-'od-gźon-nur-gyur-pa-la bka'-stsal-pa / gźon-nu de-lta-bas-na byaṅ-chub-sems-dpa' sems-dpa'-chen-po tiṅ-ṅe-'dzin 'di 'dod-pa daṅ myur-du bla-na-med-pa yaṅ-dag-par-rdzogs-pa'i byaṅ-chub mṅon-par-rdzogs-par-'tschaṅ-rgya-bar 'dod-pas lus-daṅ-srog-la ma-chags-par bya'o /

/ de ci'i phyir źe-na / gźon-nu lus-daṅ-srog-la chags-pa'i phyir sems-can-rnams mi-dge-ba'i las-mṅon-par-'du-byed-par 'gyur-ro //

// gźon-nu byaṅ-chub-sems-dpa' sems-dpa'-chen-po lus-daṅ-srog-la ma-chags-pa-rnams-la ni bla-na-med-pa yaṅ-dag-par-rdzogs-pa'i byaṅ-chub kyaṅ rñed-par mi-dka'-na tiṅ-ṅe-'dzin 'di-lta ci-smos / gźon-nu de-lta-bas-

---

1) B °theḥ. 2) C mahāsatvenaimaṃ, B *om.* bodhisatvena. 3) C samādhikām ākāṃkṣatā. 4) C *ad.* kāmena. 5) A cānavadhyav°. 6) c. T.; AD °hetor hi bodhisatvānām akuśalaḥ, B °heto hi kumāra bodhisatvena mahāsatvenâkuśalaḥ, C hetor hi kumāra bodhisatvānām akuśalaḥ. 7) AD *om.* 8) B durlabhavaty.

tvayā[1]) kumāra sadā śikṣitavyam[2]). tatredam ucyate:

na lus-daṅ-srog-la yaṅ ma-chags-par-bya'o źes de-ltar khyod-kyis bslab-par-bya'o / de-la 'di-skad ces bya-ste //

4) adhyavasāna[3]) karitvana[4]) bālā / pūtiki kāyi aśāśvati nitye / jīviti caiv' avalaṃbiya[5]), pāpaṃ / kurviṣu[6]) nity' abudhāḥ[7]) sukhahetoḥ. /

// rtag-tu khor-mor rnag-gi lus 'di-la / byis-pa-rnams ni rab-tu-chags byed-do / srog-la 'ju-źiṅ bde-ba - 'dod-pa'i phyir / mi-mkhas-pa-dag rtag-tu sdig-pa byed //

5) yeṣa[8]) na vidyati adhyavasāno / kāyi asāriki jīviti caiva / te nihanitvana māracamūnāṃ[9]) / bodhivaṭasmi[10]) prabudhyiṣu[11]) bodhim. /

// su-dag sñiṅ-po-med-pa'i lus-srog-la / lhag-par-chags-pa yod-pa ma-yin-pa / de-dag-gis ni bdud-kyi sde bcom-ste / byaṅ-chub-śiṅ-druṅ byaṅ-chub rab-tu-rtogs //

6) ye puna kāyi nirātmaki[12]) śūnye[13]) / jīviti svapnanibhe cali 'vaśye[14]) / adhyavasāna ubhe pi karonti / te cyuta yānti narā narakānī[15]). /

// su-dag bdag-med stoṅ-pa'i lus-rnams daṅ / srog kyaṅ rmi-lam gyo-ba zil-pa 'dra / 'di gñis-la ni chags-par-byed-'gyur-ba / de-dag śi-'phos sems-can dmyal-bar-'gro //

// lus-ṅes-par-bstan-pa'i le'u-ste ñi-śu-gñis-pa'o //

XXIII.

7) tatra Bhagavān punar api Candraprabhaṃ Kumārabhūtam āmantrayate sma. tasmāt tarhi kumāra bodhisatvena mahāsatvenemaṃ samādhim ākāṃkṣatā[16])

// de-nas bcom-ldan-'das-kyis zla-'od-gźon-nur-gyur-pa-la bka'-stsal-pa / gźon-nu de-lta-bas-na byaṅ-chub-sems-dpa' sems-dpa'-chen-po tiṅ-ṅe-'dzin 'di 'dod-pa

---

[1]) D *om.* [2]) D ⁰vyaḥ. [3]) D adhyavasāne. [4]) B ⁰nā. [5]) AD avalambiṣa, B avalambi. [6]) B kurviku. [7]) AD nityavraṇaḥ. [8]) BC eṣa. [9]) BC camūnī. [10]) A ⁰tasmi, C ⁰ṭesmi. [11]) AD prabudhyiya, BC pramuddhiya. [12]) A nirātmiki, BC narātmiki. [13]) C śrūnye. [14]) AD veśe, B vesyai, C vasyai. [15]) AD narā narakālīṃ, BC nagarakānī. [16]) B mākakṣatā, C aṃkṣatā.

kṣipraṃ cânuttarāṃ samyaksaṃbodhim abhisaṃboddhukāmena na rūpakāyatas tathāgataḥ prajñātavyaḥ.[1]) tat kasya hetoḥ? dharmakāyaprabhāvitāś ca buddhā bhagavanto[2]) na rūpakāyaprabhāvitāḥ.

8) tatra kumāra bodhisatvena mahāsatvena[3]) tathāgatakāyaṃ prārthayitukāmena[4]) tathāgatakāyaṃ jñātukāmenâyaṃ[5]) samādhir udgrahītavyaḥ paryavāptavyo dhārayitavyo vācayitavyaḥ pravarttayitavya[6]) uddeṣṭavyaḥ[7]) svādhyātavyo bhāvanāyogam anuyuktena[8]) ca bhavitavyaṃ parebhyaś ca vistareṇa saṃprakāśayitavyaḥ[9]).

9) tatra kumāra[10]) tathāgatakāyaḥ [11]) śatapuṇyanirjātayā [12]) buddhyā ekārthanirdeśo[13])dharmanirjāto animittaḥ[14]) sarvanimittāpagato gaṃbhīro apramāṇo apramāṇadharmo animittasvabhāvaḥ sarvanimittavibhāvito acalo apratiṣṭhito atyantākāśasvabhāvo adṛśyaś cakṣuḥpathasamatikrānto[15]) dharmakāyaḥ prajñātavyaḥ.

daṅ myur-du bla-na-med-pa yaṅ-dag-par-rdzogs-pa'i byaṅ-chub mṅon-par-rdzogs-par-'tshaṅ-rgya-bar-'dod-pas de-bźin-gśegs-pa gzugs-kyi skur mi blta'o / de ci'i phyir źe-na / saṅs-rgyas bcom-ldan-'das-rnams ni chos-kyi skus rab-tu-phye-ba yin-te gzugs-kyi skus rab-tu-phye-ba ma-yin-no //

// gźon-nu de-la byaṅ-chub-sems-dpa' sems-dpa'-chen-po de-bźin-gśegs-pa'i sku-la smon-par-'dod-pa daṅ / de-bźin-gśegs-pa'i sku śes-par-'dod-pas tiṅ-ṅe-'dzin 'di gzuṅ-bar-bya / kun-chub-par-bya / bcaṅ-par-bya / klag-par-bya / rab-tu-ldon-par-bya / luṅ-mnod-ciṅ kha-ton-du-bya / bsgom-par-bya bsgom-pa'i sbyor-ba-la rjes-su-brtson-par-bya / gźan-la yaṅ rgya-cher rab-tu-bstan-par bya'o //

// gźon-nu de-bźin-gśegs-pa'i sku ni bsod-nams-brgya-pa-las-skyes-pa'i blo daṅ don-gcig-tu-bstan-pa yin-te / chos-la skyes-pa / mtshan-ma-med-pa / mtshan-ma-thams-cad-daṅ-bral-ba / zab-pa /tshad-med-pa / tshad-med-pa'i chos / mtshan-ma-med-pa'i ṅo-bo-ñid / mtshan-ma-thams cad-rnam-par-bśig-pa / mi-gyo-ba / mi-

[1]) D prajñayate. [2]) BC *ad.* dharmakāyaprabhāvitaś ca. [3]) A *om.* mahāsatvena. [4]) A pratyapayitu⁰. [5]) B kămenāya. [6]) B *ad.* deśayitavyaḥ. [7]) C urddeśaḥ *and om. the rest of the §.* [8]) A anuyuktana. [9]) B saṃprakāsaṃprakāsayitavyaḥ. [10]) D kumāra tatra, C *om. the whole beginning down to* ekārthanirdeśo. [11]) B tathāgatasya kāyaḥ, D tathāgatakāyaḥ yaḥ. [12]) AD ⁰niryātayā. [13]) AD buddhyānekārtha⁰, B buddhyākārtha⁰. [14]) B ānimitta. [15]) BC cakṣuḥprathamamatikrāntaḥ.

10) acintyaś cittabhūmivigamaḥ sukhaduḥkhaviprakampyaḥ[1]) sarvaprapañcasamatikrānto aniketo[2]) buddhajñānaṃ prārthayitukāmānāṃ[3]) ghoṣasamatikrāntaḥ, sārago[4])rāgasamatikrāntaḥ[5]), abhedyo[6]) doṣasamatikrāntaḥ, [dhruvo mohasamatikrāntaḥ][7]),

11) nirdiṣṭaḥ śūnyatānirdeśena,[8]) ajāto jātisamatikrānto, nityo vyāhāreṇa, nirviśeṣo[9]) nirvāṇena, nirvṛtaḥ śabdena, śānto[10]) ghoṣena, sāmānyaḥ saṃketena, saṃketaḥ paramārthena, paramārtho yathābhūtavacanena,

12) śītalo niṣparidāhaḥ[11]), aniketo, amanyito, anindito, aparyanto varṇanirdeśena[12]), mahābhijñāparikarmanirjāto 'yaṃ sa ucyate kumāra tathāgatakāya iti.

gnas-pa/śin-tu-nam-mkha'i ṅo-bo-ñid / mi-snaṅ-ba / mig-gi-lam-las yaṅ-dag-par-'das-pa ni chos-kyi-skur rab-tu-śes-par-bya-ste //

//bsam-gyis-mi-khyab-pa /bsam-pa'i-sa-daṅ-bral-ba / bde-ba-daṅ-sdug-bsṅal-gyis mi-bskyod-pa / spros-pa thams-cad-las yaṅ-dag-par-'das-pa / gnas-med-pa / saṅs-rgyas-kyi ye-śes-la smon-par-'dod-pa - rnams-kyi sgra-las śin-tu-'das-pa'i sñiṅ-po-ste 'dod-chags-las-yaṅ-dag-par-'das-pa / dbyer-mi-phyed-pa-ste że-sdaṅ-las-yaṅ-dag-par-'das-pa / brtan-pa-ste gti-mug-las-yaṅ-dag-par-'das-pa /

/ stoṅ-pa-ñid-du-bstan-pas ṅes-par-bstan-pa / ma-skyes-pa skye-ba-las-yaṅ-dag-par-'das-pa / tha-sñad-du brtags-pa / mya-ṅan-las-'das-pa bye-brag-med-pa/ sgrasmya-ṅan-las-'das-pa/ dbyaṅs kyis źi-ba / brdas mtshuṅs-par-gyur-pa /don-dam-pas brdar-gyur-pa / yaṅ-dag-pa-ji-lta-ba'i tshig-gis don-dam-pa /

/ yoṅs-su-gduṅ-ba-med-pas bsil-ba / gnas-med-pa / gźal-du-med-pa / kha-dog-bstan-pas mu-med-pa / mṅon-par-śes-pa-chen-po yoṅs-su-sbyoṅ-ba-las-byuṅ-ba-ste / gźon-nu de-ni de-bźin-gśegs-pa'i sku źes bya'o //

---

1) B °vipavapyaḥ. 2) D om. 3) B pārthayitukāmānāṃ, C prāthayikāmānāṃ. 4) c. T.: A saroge, B sarāśā, C sarāgo, D sarāga. 5) C raga°. 6) C abheyo, B abheyyo. 7) c. T, Ch.: Mss. om. dhruvo mohasamatikrāntaḥ. 8) B nirdisena. 9) B niviṣeṣyo, C nirviṣeso. 10) B sānte. 11) B nipāridāhaḥ, C niḥparidahaḥ. 12) D °deśana.

13) atha khalu Bhagavāṃs tasyāṃ velāyām [1]) imā [2]) gāthā abhāṣata:

ya icchel lokanāthasya / kāyaṃ jānitum īdṛśam/ imaṃ samādhiṃ[3]) bhāvetu [4]) / kāyaṃ buddhasya jñāsyati. /

14) puṇyanirjātu buddhasya / śuddhaḥ kāyaḥ prabhāsvaraḥ / sameti so 'ntarikṣeṇa / nānātvaṃ nâsya labhyate.[5]) /

15) yādṛśā bodhi buddhasya[6]) / lakṣaṇāni ca tādṛśā / yādṛśā lakṣaṇā [7]) tasya / tasya kāyo pi tādṛśāḥ. /

16) sambodhilakṣaṇaḥ [8]) kāyo / buddhakṣetraṃ pi tādṛśaṃ [9]) / balā vimokṣā dhyānāni / sarve te py ekalakṣaṇāḥ. [10]) /

17) evaṃ sambhava [11]) buddhānāṃ / lokanāthāna[12]) īdṛśaḥ / na jātu kenacic chakyaṃ / paśyituṃ māṃsacakṣuṣā [13]). /

18) bahū [14]) evaṃ pravakṣyanti [15]) / dṛṣṭo me lokanāyakaḥ / suvarṇavarṇaḥ kāyena / sarvalokaṃ prabhāsati. /

19) adhiṣṭhānena buddhānam / anubhāvād vikurvitaiḥ / yenâ-

// de-nas bcom-ldan-'das-kyis de'i tshe tshigs-su-bcad-pa 'di-dag gsuṅs-so //

// 'di-'dra'i jig-rten-mgon-po'i sku / su-dag śes-par 'dod-pa ni / tiṅ-'dzin 'di ni bsgom-gyis daṅ / saṅs-rgyas-sku ni śes-par-'gyur //

// saṅs-rgyas-sku ni dag-paste / bsod-nams-brgya-skyes 'od-kyaṅ-gsal / de ni bar-snaṅ mtshuṅs-pa-ste / de-la tha-dad bya-ba-med //

// saṅs-rgyas-byaṅ-chub ci-'draba / mtshan-rnams kyaṅ ni de-'dra-ste / de-yi mtshan-rnams ci-'dra-ba / de-yi sku yaṅ de-'dra'o //

// sku ni byaṅ chub-msthan-ñid de / saṅs-rgyas-źiṅ yaṅ de-'dra źiṅ / stobs daṅ rnam-thar bsam-gtan yaṅ / de-dag thams-cad mtshan-ñid-gcig //

//de-ltar saṅs-rgyas-'byun 'gyur-te / 'jig-rten-mgon-po'i de-'dra-bas / sus-kyaṅ śa-yi mig-gis ni / nam-yaṅ mthoṅ-bar mi-nus-so //

// maṅ-po-dag kyaṅ 'di skad smra / ṅas ni 'jig-rten-'dren-pa mthoṅ / sku yaṅ gser-gyi kha-dog-la / 'jig-rten thams-cad snaṅ-bar-mdzad //

// saṅs-rgyas-dag-gi byin-brlabs daṅ / mthu daṅ rnam-thar-

---

[1]) B vyelāyāṃ. [2]) BC imāṃ. [3]) B samādhi. [4]) D bhāvet tu. [5]) DC labhate [6]) AD satvasya. [7]) D yādṛśaṃ lakṣaṇaṃ. [8]) BC °ṇāḥ. [9]) B °kṣetra pi tādṛśaḥ. [10]) BC °ṇ̆ḥ [11]) BC sarva, D sambha. [12]) B lokanātha. [13]) B °ṣă [14]) B bahūṃ. [15]) D pravekṣyanti.

sau [1]) dṛśyate kāyo / lakṣaṇehi vicitritaḥ[2]) /

20) ārohapariṇāhena / kāyo buddhasya deśitaḥ / na ca pramānaṃ kāyasya / labdhaṃ tena acintiyaḥ. /

21) yadi pramāṇaṃ labhyeta/ kāyo buddhasya ettako [3]) / nirviśeṣo bhavec chāstā / devaiś ca manujair api. /

22) samāhitasya cittasya / vipāko pi tallakṣaṇaḥ [4]) / tallakṣaṇaṃ nāma-rūpaṃ / śuddhaṃ bhoti prabhāsvaram [5]). /

23) na caiṣa [6]) kenacij jātu [7]) / samādhiḥ śāntu bhāvitaḥ / yatheha lokanāthena / kalpakoṭyo niṣevitaḥ [8]). /

24) bahubhiḥ śukladharmaiś ca/ samādhir janito hy ayaṃ / samādher asya vaipulyāt [9]) / kāyo mahyan na dṛśyate. /

25) yasya vo yādṛśaṃ cittaṃ/ nāma-rūpaṃ pi tādṛśaṃ[10])/ nisvabhāvasya cittasya [11]) / nāmarūpaṃ tallakṣaṇam. /

26) yasya codāra saṃjñādi [12]) / nāma-rūpasmi varttate / visabhāgāya saṃjñāya / udāraṃ[13]) cittu jāyate, /

sprul-pa-yis / de-ltar mtshan-gyis spras-pa-yi / sku-dag śin-tu-snaṅ-ba yin //

// boṅ-tshod khrun daṅ sboms-su yaṅ / saṅs-rgyas-sku ni bśad-mod-kyis / sku-yi tshad ni ma-rñed-do / de-phyir bsam-gyis-mi-khyab-bo //

// saṅs-rgyas-sku ni 'di-tsam źes / gal-te tshad kyaṅ rñed-gyur-na / lha-dag daṅ ni mi-rnams daṅ/ ston-pa bye-brag-med-par-'gyur//

// mñam - par-bźag-pa'i sems-kyi[14]) ni/rnam-par-smin-pa'aṅ de-yi mtshan / miṅ-daṅ-gzugs kyaṅ de-'dra-mtshan /rnam-par-dag-ciṅ 'od-gsal-'gyur //

// ji-ltar 'jig-rten-mgon-po-yis / bskal-pa-bye-bar bsñen-pa ltar / sus-kyaṅ tiṅ-'dzin źi-ba 'di/nam-yaṅ gnas-par ma-byas - so //

dkar-po'i chos ni maṅ-po-yis / tiṅ-'dzin 'di ni bskyed-pa-ste / tiṅ-'dzin 'di ni rgya-che-bas /ṅa-yi lus kyaṅ mi snaṅ-ṅo //

// gaṅ-gi sems ni ci-'dra-ba / miṅ-daṅ-gzugs kyaṅ de-'dra-ste/ raṅ-bźin-med-pa'i sems-kyi ni / miṅ-daṅ-gzugs kyaṅ mtshan-de-'dra //

// miṅ-daṅ-gzugs-la gaṅ-gi ni/ 'du-śes rags-pa [15]) 'jug-pa yaṅ/ skal-pa [16])-mi-mñam 'du-śes-kyis/ rags-pa'i sems kyaṅ skye-bar-'gyur //

---

[1]) A yena so B yenâsā, C yenāsau. [2]) BC °tāḥ. [3]) BC etako. [4]) C *om.* [5]) B °raḥ. [6]) BC caiṣaḥ. [7]) BC jātuḥ. [8]) B niṣeviḥ [9]) B samādhir asya vaipulyā. [10]) A °rūpe pi tādṛśe [11]) BC *om.* [12]) A °ādir. [13]) A udāra. [14]) Mss. kyis. [15]) P rigs-pa. [16]) P bskal-pa.

27) yasya ca mṛdukī saṃjñā / nāma-rūpasmi varttate / agṛddhaṃ [1]) nāma-rūpasmi [2]) / cittaṃ bhoti prabhāsvaram./	// miṅ-daṅ-gzugs-la su-dag-gi / 'du-śes phra-mo 'jug-pa ni / miṅ-daṅ-gzugs-la ma-chags-pas/ sems ni rab-tu-'od-gsal-'gyur //
28) smarāmy ahaṃ pūrvajātīṣv / asaṃkhyeyeṣu saptasu [3]) / tisro[4]) me pāpikāḥ saṃjñā [5]) / naivotpannāḥ kadācanā. /	// ṅas dran sṅon-gyi tshe-rabs ni / graṅs-med-pa-dag bdun-du yaṅ / sdig-pa'i 'du-śes gsum-po-dag / nam-yaṅ skyes-par ma-gyur-to //
29) anāsravaṃ ca me cittaṃ / kalpakoṭyo [6]) hy acintiyāḥ [7]) / karomi cârthaṃ satvānāṃ / na ca me kāyu [8]) dṛśyate. /	// ṅa-yi sems ni zag-med-do / bskal-pa bye [16])-ba bsam-yas-su/ sems-can-rnams-kyi don byed kyaṅ / ṅa-yi lus ni mi-snaṅ-ṅo //
30) yathā ca yasya bhāvehi / vimuktaṃ bhoti mānasaṃ / na tasya tehi bhāvehi / bhūyo bhoti samāgamaḥ. /	// ji-ltar gaṅ-gi dṅos-po-las / yid kyaṅ rnam-par-grol-gyur-pa / de-dag de-yi dṅos-po daṅ / phyir-yaṅ phrad-par mi-'gyur-ro //
31) vimuktam mama vijñānaṃ / sarvabhāvehi sarvaśaḥ / svabhāvo jñātu cittasya / bhūyo jñānaṃ pravarttate /	// dṅos-po kun-las rnam-pa-kun / ṅa-yi rnam-śes rnam-grol-te/ sems-kyi raṅ-bźin śes-pas-na / phyir-yaṅ ye-śes 'byuṅ-bar-'gyur //
32) kṣetra-koṭi-sahasrāṇi / gacchanti mama nirmitāḥ [9])/kurvanti cârthaṃ [10]) satvānāṃ / yatra kāyo na labhyate. /	// źiṅ-rnams bye-ba phrag-stoṅ-du / ṅa-yi sprul-pa-dag kyaṅ 'gro/ sems-can-rnams-kyi don kyaṅ byed / de-la lus kyaṅ rñed [17]) mi-'gyur //
33) alakṣaṇo nirnimitto [11]) / yathaiva gaganaṃ tathā / kāyo nirabhilāpyo me / durvijñeyo [12]) nidarśitaḥ./	// mtshan-ñid-med-ciṅ mtshan-ma-med / ji-ltar nam-mkha' de-bźin-du / ṅa-yi sku yaṅ brjod-med-ciṅ / śes-par-dka'-bar rab-tu-bstan //
34) dharmakāyo mahāvīro / dharmeṇa [13]) kāyu [14]) nirjito [15]) /	// dpa'-bo-chen-po chos-kyi sku / sku-ni chos-las skyes-pa-ste/

---

1) AD agṛddhram. 2) BC *om.* varttate agṛddhaṃ nāmarūpasmi. 3) B suptasu. 4) BC trisro. 5) D jñaṃjñā. 6) B °koṭi. 7) D acintitaḥ. 8) BC kāya. 9) AD nirvṛtāḥ, B nimitāḥ. 10) B °tha 11) A nirminitto, BC ninirmittā. 12) C °vijñayo. 13) B dharmaṇo. 14) BC kāya. 15) A nirjivo. 16) P bya. 17) P dñed.

na jātu rūpakāyena / śakyaṃ prajñāpituṃ[1]) jino[2]). /

35) kathā nirdeśu[3])yasyaitaṃ[4]) / śrutvā prītir[5]) bhaviṣyati / na tasya Mārah pāpīyān/avatāraṃ[6]) labhiṣyati. /

36) śrutvā ca dharmaṃ gaṃbhīraṃ[7]) / yasya[8]) trāso na[9]) bheṣyati/na câsau jīvitārthāya[10]) / buddhabodhiṃ pratikṣipet /

37) sūtra[11])-koṭī-sahasrāṇāṃ / bhūtanirdeśu[12]) jñāsyati / ālokabhūto[13]) lokānāṃ / yena yena gamiṣyati[14]) /

38) tatra[15]) kumāra tathāgatasya kāyaḥ nimittakarmaṇâpi[16]) na sukaraṃ jñātum. nīlo vā, nīlavarṇo vā, nīlanidarśano va, nīlanirbhāso vā.

pīto vā°...
lohito vā°...
avadāto vā°...
mañjiṣṭho vā°...
sphaṭiko vā°...

agneyo vā, agnivarṇo vā, agni°...
sarpimaṇḍopamo[17]) vā, sarpirvarṇo vā, sarpir°...
sauvarṇo vā, suvarṇavarṇo vā°...
vaiḍūryo vā°...[18])

gzugs-kyi skur ni nam-du-yaṅ/ rgyal-ba gdags-par yod mi-nus //

// ji-ltar bśad-pa 'di-dag kyaṅ/ thos-nas dga'-bar 'gyur-ba ni/ de-la sdig-can bdud-kyis kyaṅ / glags-pa[19]) rñed-par mi-'gyur-ro //

// zab-mo-yi ni chos thos-nas/ de-la skrag-pa mi-'byuṅ-ste / de ni[20]) srog-gi phyir-du yaṅ /saṅs-rgyas byaṅ-chub spoṅ mi byed//

// mdo-sde bye-ba phrag-stoṅ-gi/yaṅ-dag-bstan-pa śes-par-'gyur/ gaṅ-du[21]) gaṅ-du soṅ-bar yaṅ / 'jig-rten-dag-la snaṅ-bar-'gyur //

// gźon-nu de-la de-bźin-gśegs-pa'i sku ni mtshan-ma-daṅ-las-kyis kyaṅ śes-par sla-ba ma-yin-te / sṅon-po-'am / kha-dog sṅon po-'am / sṅon-po lta-bur-ston-pa-'am / 'od sṅon-po'byuṅ-ba'am/

ser-po-'am°...
dmar-po-'am °...
dkar-po 'am °...
le-brgan-nam °...
śel-lam / śel-gyi kha-dog-gam / śel lta-bur-ston pa-'am / śel-gyi 'od 'byuṅ-ba °...

me-'am / me'i kha-dog °...
mar-gyi sñiṅ-po-'am/mar-gyi kha-dog-gam / mar-lta-bur °...
gser-ram / gser-gyi kha-dog °...
bai-ḍu[22])-rya-'am / bai-ḍu[22])-rya'i kha-dog °...

[1]) D prajñāpayitum. [2]) D janaḥ. [3]) BC nirdeṣṭu, D nirdeśa. [4]) D tasyaivam. [5]) BC prīti. [6]) B avatāra. [7]) BC gambhīrasya. [8]) BC *om.* [9]) B so. [10]) B °thaya, C °thāyā. [11]) A *om. the whole stanza.* [12]) B bhūtan nirdeṣṭu, CD bhūtan nirdeśu. [13]) B °bhūta. [14]) C °ṣyanti. [15]) A *om. the whole beginning down to* jñātum. [16]) c.T.; Mss. °karmāpi. [17]) A sarpirmaṇḍopamo, BC sarpimaṃtopamo. [18]) A vaiduryo, B vainduryo. [19]) Mss. glan-ka. [20]) P na. [21]) N dag. [22]) P dū.

vidyud vā°...
brahmo vā°...

glog-gam / glog-gi kha-dog-gam°.., tshaṅs-pa-'am / tshaṅs-pa'i kha-dog-gam °...

devo vā, devavarṇo vā, devani darśano vā, devanirbhāso vā iti hi[1]) kumāra tathāgatasya kāyaḥ śuddho [2]), nimittenâpy acintyaḥ, acintyanirdeśaḥ, sarvanimittair [3]) apy acintyaḥ, acintyanidarśanaḥ[4]),

lha-'am / lha'i kha-dog-gam / lha lta-bur-ston-pa - 'am / lha'i 'od 'byun-ba'o źes ses-par sla-ba ma-yin-no / gźon-nu de-ltar de-bźin-gśegs-pa'i sku ni dag-pa-ste / mtshan-ma-dag-gis bsam-par bya-ba ma-yin-pa / bsam-gyis mi-khyab-par bstan-pa / mtshan-ma thams-cad-kyis kyaṅ bsam-par bya-ba ma-yin-pa / bsam- gyis mi-khyab-par bstan-pa-ste /

39) rūpakāyapariniṣpattyā[5]) na sukaraṃ sadevakenâpi lokena [6]) kāyasya pramāṇam udgrahītum anyatra sarvākārair acintyo aprameyaḥ.

/ rnam-pa thams-cad bsam-gyis mi-khyab-ciṅ dpag-tu-med-pa źes bya-ba ma-gtogs-par lha-daṅ-bcas-pa'i 'jig-rten-gyis kyaṅ gzugs-kyi sku yoṅs-su-rdzogs-pas sku'i tshad gzuṅ-bar sla ma-yin-no //

40) atha khalu Bhagavān tasyāṃ velāyām imā [7]) gāthā abhāṣata:
yad rajo [8]) lokadhātūṣu / pāṃsusamjñā-nidarśanam / utsa-hrada[9])-taḍāgeṣu / samudreṣu ca yaj jalaṃ /

// de-nas bcom-ldan-'das-kyis de'i tshe tshigs-su bcad-pa 'di-dag gsuṅs-so //
// 'jig-rten-khams-kyi rdul-phran daṅ/ rdul-du-miṅ yaṅ ston-pa daṅ/ mtshe'u daṅ rdziṅ daṅ lteṅ-ka daṅ / rgya-mtsho-na yaṅ ji-sñed chu //

41) na teṣaṃ labhyate anto / ettakā[10]) paramāṇavaḥ. / samudrād vālakoṭībhir[11]) / mātuṃ śakyaṃ jalaṃ [12]) bhavet, /
42) na tulyā [13]) lokanāthena /

// 'di-sñed rdul-phran yod-do źes / de-dag-la ni mtha' mi-rñed / rgya-mtsho-la ni skra-rtse[14])-yis/ chu-thigs gźal-bar nus kyaṅ ni //
// 'jig-rten-mgon-po'i dpe-ñid-

---

[1]) CD *om.* [2]) c. T.: Mss. śuddha. [3]) D sarvanidarśair. [4]) AD °nirdeśo. [5]) A rūpakāyaniṣkattya, BC rūpakāyapariniṣapasyā, D rūpakāyaniṣpattyā [6]) BC *ad.* na. [7]) BC imāṃ [8]) B rañja. [9]) A dahrada. [10]) B etatka, C etako. [11]) B °koṭitipra. [12]) B jā!aṃ. [13]) AD tu yo, B tu yāval, C tu yā. [14]) N rtsa.

upanā saṃprakāśitā. / jalabindavo aprameyās [1]) / tathaiva paramāṇavaḥ, /

43) paśyāmy ekasya satvasya [2])/ tato bahutarān aham / adhimukti [3])-citta-utpādo / naikakāle [4]) prajānitum. /

44) ye mayā ātmabhāvasya / bhūtavarṇā nidarśitāḥ / sarvasatvā 'dhimuktās tān / eteṣām upamā[5]) 'kṣamāḥ. /

45) nimittakarmaṇā naiva / varṇanirbhāsa īdṛśaḥ / śakyaṃ jānituṃ buddhasya / viśeṣo hîdṛśo mama [6]). /

46) nimittāpagatā buddhā / dharmakāyaprabhāvitāḥ / gaṃbhīrāś câprameyāś ca / tena buddhā acintiyāḥ [7]). /

47) acintiyasya [8]) buddhasya / buddhakāyo py acintiyaḥ [9]) / acintiyā hi te[10]) kāyā [11]) / dharmakāyaprabhāvitāḥ. /

48) cittenâpi na buddhānāṃ / kāyaṃ cintayituṃ kṣamaḥ[12]) / tathā hi tasya kāyasya / pramāṇaṃ nopalabhyate. /

49) aprameyā hi te dharmāḥ / kalpakoṭyo niṣevitāḥ / tena [13]) acintiyaḥ [14]) kāyo / nirvṛto me prabhāsvaraḥ. /

50) agrāhyaḥ sarvasatvehi / na pramāṇena gṛhyate / tathā hi

du/ yaṅ-dag-bstan-par mi-ruṅ-ṅo/ chu-yi thigs-pa dpag-med-ciṅ/ de-bźin rab-tu-phra-ba'i rdul //

// de-bas sems-can gcig gi yaṅ śin-tu-maṅ-du ṅas mthoṅ-ste/ mos-pa daṅ ni sems-bskyed-pa/ du-ma-dag ni śes-mi-sla //

// ṅas ni sku-yi yon-tan-dag / yaṅ-dag-pa ni gaṅ bstan-pa / sems-can-kun-gyi mos-pa yaṅ / de-dag dpe-ru bzod mi-'gyur //

// mtshan-ma daṅ ni las-rnams daṅ / kha-dog-snaṅ-pa 'di-'dra źes / saṅs-rgyas kyi ni śes mi-nus / ṅa-yi bye-brag de-'dra'o //

// saṅs-rgyas mtshan-ma-bral-ba-ste / chos-kyi sku-yis rab-tu/ phye / zab-ciṅ dpag-tu-med-pa-ste/ de-phyir saṅs-rgyas bsam-mi-khyab //

// saṅs-rgyas bsam-du-med-pa-yi/saṅs-rgyas-sku yaṅ bsam-du-med / sku de bsam-du-med-pa-yi / chos-kyi sku-yis rab-tu-phye //

// saṅs-rgyas-sku ni sems-kyis kyaṅ / bsam-par bzod-pa ma-yin-te / de-ltar de-yi sku-la yaṅ / tshad kyaṅ ñe-bar-mi-dmigs-so //

// chos-rnams de-dag dpag-tu-med / bskal-pa bye-bar bsñen-pas-na / de-phyir ṅa-yi lus kyaṅ ni/'od-gsal bsam-du-med-pa grub//

// sems-can kun-gyis gzuṅ-du-med / tshad-kyis gzuṅ-bya ma-

---

[1]) BC prameyās. [2]) BC ekasatvasya. [3]) B apimukti, D adhimukta. [4]) BC nekakāle. [5]) c. T, Ch; Mss. upāgamāḥ. [6]) A mayā, BC mamaḥ. [7]) D acintitāḥ. [8]) D acintitasya. [9]) D acintitaḥ. [10]) A acintiyo hi ta, B acintya hi te, C acintyo hi te, D acintita hi te. [11]) c. T. Ch.; Mss. kāma. [12]) A kṣayaḥ. [13]) Mss. teno. [14]) BC acintyaḥ, D acintitaḥ.

kāyo buddhasya / apramāṇo [1]) acintiyaḥ[2])

51) apramāṇehi[3]) dharmehi / pramāṇaṃ tatra kalpate[4]) / akalpitehi dharmehi [5]) / buddho py evam akalpitaḥ [6]) /

52) pramāṇaṃ kalpam ākhyāto[7]) / apramāṇam akalpitam [8]) / akalpyaḥ kalpāpagatas [9]) / tena buddho acintiyaḥ [10]) /

53) apramāṇaṃ yathâkāśaṃ[11]) / mātuṃ śakyaṃ na kenacit / tathaiva [12]) kāyu [13]) buddhasya / ākāśasamasādṛśaḥ /

54) ye kāyam evaṃ jānanti / buddhānāṃ te jinātmajāḥ / te pi buddhā bhaviṣyanti /lokanāthā [14]) acintiyāḥ [15]). /

iti tathāgatakāyanirdeśaparivartto nāma dvaviṃśatitamaḥ.

yin-te/de-ltar[16])saṅs-rgyas-sku-dag ni / tshad-med bsam-gyis-mi-khyab-pa //

// tshad-med-pa-yi chos-dag-gis / de-la tshad ni brtag-tu-med / ma-brtags-pa-yi[17]) chos-dag-gis[18])/ de-ltar saṅs-rgyas bsam-du-med //

// rtog-pa-dag [19]) ni tshad-du-bstan / rtog-pa-med-pa tshad-med yin / mi-rtog rtog-daṅ-bral-bas-na / de-phyir saṅs - rgyas bsam - du med //

// ji-ltar nam-mkha' tshad-med-la / sus-kyaṅ gźal-du mi-nus-pa / de-bźin saṅs-rgyas-sku-dag kyaṅ / nam-mkha'-ñid [20]) daṅ 'dra - źiṅ mtshuṅs //

// saṅs-rgyas-sku ni de-lta-bur / gaṅ-gis rig-pa rgyal-ba' i sras / de-dag bsam-gyis-mi-khyab-pa / saṅs-rgyas 'jig-rten-mgon-por gyur //

// de-bźin-gśegs-pa'i sku ṅes-pai -bstan-pa'i le'u-ste ñi-śu-gsum-pa'o //

---

1) C pramāṇo. 2) D acintitaḥ. 3) BC °ṇo hi. 4) AD kalpyate, C kalapate. 5) B *om.* 6) A acintiyaḥ. 7) BC ākhy°. 8) A akalpiyam. 9) AD °apagas. 10) D acintitaḥ. 11) AD yathā kāyam, B yathâkāsa. 12) A tathaivo. 13) *c metri causa;* Mss. kāyo 14) B °thā. 15) D acintitāḥ. 16) N lta. 17) P le. 18) Mss. gi. 19) N dge. 20) P ñed.

TRANSLATION

VIII.

1) Then the Lord spoke anew to the princely Candraprabha [41]): — "Therefore, o Kumāra, the Bodhisattva-Mahāsattva who strives for this *samādhi* and wishes to attain the Supreme Enlightenment speedily, should be an expert knower of the essence of the non-existence.

2) How, o Kumāra, does a Bodhisattva-Mahāsattva become an expert knower of the essence of the non-existence? This Bodhisattva-Mahāsattva, o Kumāra, ought to comprehend all the *dharmas* as being non-existent in their essence [42]), as signless [43]), markless [44]), not origin-

---

41) Ch. begins with the stereotyped formula (which however is often omitted): „Then the Buddha addressed the princely Candraprabha in these words..." Then follows the translation of the 8th paragraph. The §§ 1—7 are missing in Ch.

42) „of which the essence is the want of their own existence" = *abhāva-svabhāva* = *dṅos-po-med-pa'i ṅo-bo-ñid* as in K. The translation of T. *dṅos-po-med-pa / ṅo-bo-ñid-med-pa* is based on a false reading (attested in C): *abhāvā asvabhāvā*. *abhāvā*, obviously, means „want of its own existence", cf. Pr. $265_{7,8}$ and not „absence of the dharmas" as proved by the T. where the „non-being" is generally rendered by the words *med-pa*, *ye-med*, etc., and *dṅos-po-med-pa* can denote only the „want of an absolute existence". Cf. Th. Stcherbatsky, *Die drei Richtungen in der Philosophie des Buddhismus*, RO, X, p. 20, foot-note 3.

43) K.: *mtshan-ma-med-pa źes bya-ba-la / mtshan-ma ni dṅos-po'i rtags-te / mtshan-ma daṅ rtags daṅ rgyu gaṅ-gis de 'dzin-pa-ñid-do // mo-gśam-gyi bu bźin-du ma-skyes-pa-ñid-la ni mtshan-ma'i ṅo-bo-med-pas mtshan-ma-med-pa-ñid-do//*= „signless. The sing is the attribute of existence. How the perception *('dzin-pa= grahaṇa)* of the sign and of the attribute are possible? Just as the son of a barren woman cannot be born, in the same way the signs do not exist, since there is no reality for them (no reality to which these signs could be affixed)".

44) K.: *mtshan-ñid-med-pa źes bya-ba ni bya-ba'i khyad-par-gyis phuṅ-po thams-cad-kyi mtshan-ñid bstan-la // bya-ba de yaṅ gcig-pa'am/tha-dad-pa'am / gñi-ga'i ṅo-bor yaṅ med-pas mtshan-ñid daṅ mtshan-ñid-kyi raṅ-gi ṅo-bo yoṅs-su-ma-grub-pas de'i phyir mtshan-ñid-pa źes bya'o //* = „markless. By this characteristic *(khyad-par=viśeṣeṇa)* the mark of all the skandhas is determined. Both [the supposition that *lakṣaṇa* and *lakṣya=lakṣaṇa-svarūpa* are] the one and the same, and [the supposition that they are] different, these two [alternatives] are unreal; therefore, for want of proofs [of the reality] of *lakṣaṇa* and *lakṣya (mtshan-ñid-kyi raṅ-gi ṅo-bo)* it was stated: ‚markless'."

ated, nor disappearing[45]), inexpressible by letters[46]), void[47]), quiescent from the outset [48]), pure by their very nature [49]). When, o Kumāra, the Bodhisattva - Mahāsattva comprehends all the *dharmas* as being non-existent in their essence, signless, markless, etc......, then this Bodhisattva-Mahāsattva, o Kumāra, is rightly called an expert knower of the essence of the non-existence.

---

[45]) *ma-skyes-pa źes bya-ba ni raṅ daṅ/gźan daṅ/gñi-ga daṅ/rgyu-med-pa-las kyaṅ skye-bar mi-'gyur źes bya-ba-la-sogs-pas rgya-cher skye-ba bkag-pa'i phyir ma-skyes-pa'o* // = „not originated. [The dharmas] do not originate from themselves, neither from another [dharma], nor from both, nor without cause etc. On account of the utter impossibility of origination they are not originated". Cf. the famous stanza of Nāgārjuna:

na svato nâpi parato na dvābhyāṃ nâpy ahetutaḥ
utpannā jātu vidyante bhāvāḥ kvacana kecana

Pr. p. 12, *Bodhicaryāvatāra*, p. 357.

Cf. further K.: *ma-'gags-pa źes bya-ba ni skye-ba-med-pa-ñid-kyis 'gag-pa yaṅ med-do // skyes-pa ni 'gags-par 'gyur-gyi ma-skyes-pa'i mo-gśam-gyi bu-la 'chi-ba-med-pa bźin-no* // = „not disappearing. As there is no origination, so there is no destruction. While a thing which is originated can disappear, a thing which is not originated [cannot disappear], just as there is no death fot the son of a barren woman".

[46]) K.: *yi-ge-med-pa źes bya-ba ni mi-'gyur-ba brjod-du-med-pa-ste / yi-ge'i ṅo-bo ma-yin-pas sgra'i tshaṅs-pa-smra-ba-rnams-kyis yoṅs-su-brtags-pa'i raṅ-bzin daṅ bral-ba-ñid-do / de'i phyir yi-ge-med-pa'o* // = „inexpressible by letters. What does not exist is ineffable. As there is no reality in letters, the words [even those] which are created *(parikalpita)* by the divine voices *(tshaṅs-pa-smra=brahmasvara)* are devoid of essence. Therefore [the dharmas] are inexpressible by letters". *brahmasvara* is the voice of the Buddha teaching the Law. As for its unreality, see the foot-note 61.

[47]) K.: *stoṅ źes bya-ba ni bstan-ma-thag-pa'i spros-pa thams-cad-kyis ma-spros-pa bdag daṅ bdag-gis raṅ-gi ṅo-bo daṅ bral-ba stoṅ-pa-ñid-do* // = „void — completely free from the illusional plurality which was mentioned above; as there is no essence in [the notions] „I" and „mine", [the dharmas] are void".

[48]) K.: *gzod-ma nas źi-ba źes bya-ba ni skye-ba sṅon-ba'i mya-ṅan-las-'das-pa yod-pa ma-yin-gyi gzod-ma-ñid-nas mya-ṅan-las-'das-pa'o* // = „quiescent from the outset — [the dharmas] are suppressed from the outset, for a *nirvāṇa* which is preceded by the *saṃsāra* (= *jāti* = *skye-ba)* does not exist". This is the refutation of the Hīnayāna theory according to which the *nirvāṇa* is not identical with the *saṃsāra* and can be attained only after having annihilated the latter. Cf. *Bodhicaryāvatāra V, Ausgewählte Kapitel* p. 101, 102 and the foot-note 68.

[49]) K.: *raṅ-bźin-gyis rnam-par-dag-pa źes bya-ba ni dag-par bya-ba daṅ dag-par-byed-pa daṅ/dag-pa'i raṅ-gi ṅo-bo daṅ bral-bas chos thams-cad raṅ-bźin-gyis dag-pa'o // ci thams-cad-du ṅo-bo-med-pas de-skad brjod-par-bya-ba'am źe-na / de ni ma-yin-te / chos thams-cad de-bźin-du yoṅs-su-śes-par-bya'o // thams-cad-*

3) O Kumāra, the Bodhisattva-Mahāsattva who is an expert knower of the essence of the non-existence, is neither attracted nor repulsed nor infatuated by all the elements of sight, hearing, smell, taste and touch. For what reason? Because he does neither perceive nor apprehend this *dharma* [50]).

4) He neither perceives nor apprehends the *dharma* which is attracted, neither the *dharma* which attracts, nor the *dharma* due to which the attraction is produced; neither the *dharma* which is repulsed, nor the *dharma* which repulses, nor the *dharma* due to which the repulsion is produced; neither the *dharma* which is infatuated, nor the *dharma* which infatuates, nor the *dharma* due to which the infatuation is produced. Neither perceiving nor apprehending this *dharma*, he does not cling to all the elements of the threefold word, soon reaches this *samādhi* and speedily attains the Supreme Enlightenment. Since it is said:

> 5) Non-existent are all the *dharmas*[51]), signless, markless, not originated nor disappearing, — thus must you conceive all the *dharmas*.
>
> 6) They are all non-existent, inexpressible, void, quiescent, stainless from the outset; he who conceives the *dharmas* in this manner, is called Buddha [52]).

---

du yaṅ mṅon-par-źen-pa ni 'chiṅ-ba'i bdag-ñid yin-pa'i phyir 'khor-ba-las sgrol-bar mi-'gyur-ro // saṅs-rgyas don-du gñer-ba-rnams-kyi źes bya-ba ni lhag-ma'o // = „pure by their very nature; as the ‚cleaned', the ‚cleaning' and the ‚clean' are devoid of their own reality, all the dharmas are pure by their very nature. Should one say it, because there is no reality at all? That is not right. The dharmas [alone] should be cognized in this manner. Those who cling to everything, as their self is fettered, cannot be delivered from the *saṃsāra*. It remains to be completed *(źes bya-ba ni lhag-ma'o = ity avaśeṣam)* : [this teaching is meant] for those desiring to become Buddhas (for the Mahāyānists)".

[50]) K.: *des chos de yaṅ-dag-par-rjes-su-mi-mthoṅ źes bya-ba ni phyi-daṅ-naṅ-gi dṅos-po-rnams rjes-su-dpag-pas-so // mi-dmigs-pa źes bya-ba ni mṅon-sum-gyis-so //* = „He does not perceive those dharmas by means of inference *(anumāna)* from internal and external phenomena *(dṅos-po = bhāva)*. He does not apprehend by means of sense-perception *(pratyakṣa)*".

[51]) The first pāda of this stanza contains only 7 syllables. One could suppose an emendation *abhāvino sarvadharmāḥ* or *abhāvakāḥ sarvadharmāḥ* which howerer is not very likely.

[52]) Cf. Pr. p. 539 (the quotation not recognized by the editor):
avācā 'nakṣarāḥ sarva śūnyāḥ śāntâdinirmalāḥ
ya evaṃ jānati dharmān kumāro buddha socyate.

7) He who longs for this Mother of the Sugatas explained as the „Equality of the Absolute Essences" [52 bis]), let him meditate upon all the *dharmas* as non-existent. Then will he attain this Parent of the Victorious Ones [53]).

8) O Kumāra, let it be learnt by Thee from the following story:

This version seems to be the original one, for *avāca* agrees with *anakṣara* better than *abhāva*. Nevertheless, I have maintained the reading of all the four Mss. as attested by T. If it is a corruption of the original text, it is an old one and earlier than the T. translation.

[52 bis]) These words, transposed for metrical reasons, correspond to the definition *sarva-dharma-svabhāva-samatā-vipañcita*, cf. the foot-note 93. *mātāṃ=mātāraṃ* „the Mother", a figurative epithet of the *Prajñāpāramitā* considered as the Supreme Wisdom helping the Bodhisattvas in the realisation of their aims. *jananī*, two lines lower, has the same meaning.

[53]) This entire stanza deserves attention both for metrical and philological reasons. The variety of the *Triṣṭubh* ⏓ — ⏑ ⏑ ⏑ — ⏑ ⏑ — ⏑ — — is quite unknown in the early poetry and appears only in the Mahāyāna texts.

Prof. Helmer Smith calls my attention to the following verses of the *Saddharmapuṇḍarīkasūtra*:

III,45b *manuṣyakuṇapāni vibhakṣayantaḥ* and
III,47b *manuṣyakuṇapāni vikaḍḍhamānāḥ*

and tries to explain this innovation through the confusion of pādas. E. g. in *Saddharmapuṇḍ.* III,47ab

suraudra cittā pi vasanti yakṣa
„ „ *manuṣyakuṇapāni vikaḍḍhamānāḥ*

the poet may have connected *yakṣa* with the subsequent pāda, which gave him the familiar rhythm of *Vasantatilaka*. Such „overlapping pādas" are not unknown and may have given rise to a new kind of *Triṣṭubh*. According to this explanation, that metre can occur in pādas *b* and *d* alone. It permitted to insert into the pāda *b* of the stanza VIII,7 of the *Samādhirājasūtra* the technical term *svabhāvasamatā*, but does not suit the verse *c* of this stanza. In this pāda the reading *sa bhāvayet* would have been much better, would have corresponded more closely to the Optative *icchi* and the metre would have remained normal. Prof. H. Smith supposes that *bhāvayet* was the original reading and that *bhāvayatu* was but a gloss to it which, having been inserted into the text, was transformed into *sa bhāvayātu* (reading of A and D) by the scribe who wanted the normal initial rhythm ⏑ — ⏑ — and took no care of the superfluous syllable *-tu*.

The Mss. CD give a reading *svabhāvayatu* which can be easily explained by the influence of *svabhāva* in the preceding line. Yet, the T. translator seems to have admitted this reading, interpreting it as the Imperative of a newly formed denominative verb *svabhāvayati* which might mean: „to realize the essence [of something]". At any rate the only possibility to understand the second pāda of the T. version of this place is to replace *kyis* by *gyis*. Then *ṅo-bo-ñid-gyis*

O Kumāra [54]), formerly, in the days of yore, many immense, immeasurable, inconceivable, unfathomable [epochs], more incalculable than the „incalculable aeons" [55]) ago,—in that age there appeared on earth the Tathāgata, the Arhat, the Fully Enlightened One, Endowed with Wisdom and Virtue, the Sugata, the Knower of the World, the Supreme Guide of men who have to be restrained, the Teacher of gods and men, the Buddha and Lord, „Born of Non-existence" [56]) by name.

9) Why it is, o Kumāra, dost Thou think that this Tathāgata is called „Born of Non-existence"? O Kumāra, it is because this Tathāgata, as soon as he was born, rose up to the skies to the height of seven palmtrees and having taken seven steps uttered the following words: „All the *dharmas* are born of non-existence! All the *dharmas* are born of non-existence!" By this utterance, o Kumāra, the entire Universe containing 3 thousand thousands of worlds, was instructed [57]).

10) And starting from the terrestial gods up to the Brahma-world the following words were said and repeated from mouth to mouth [58]): „That is certainly the Tathāgata ‚Born of Non-existence', he who, as soon as he was born, rose up to the skies to the height of seven palmtrees and having taken seven steps utters the words of non-existence. He is ‚Born of Non-existence', ‚Born of Non-existence!'" Thus the name was assigned to this Lord, the Tathāgata.

11) And when the Lord had attained Enlightenment, the words „Born of Non-existence" were resounded from the leaves of all the trees, from every blade of grass, from bushes, herbs and forest-trees [59]),

---

might be considered as the Imperative of a verb *ṅo-bo-ñid-bgyid* rendering the supposed Indian denominative *svabhāvayati*. Besides, the T. version of this stanza seems corrupt and can give a somewhat satisfactory meaning only by interchanging the second and the third lines.

[54]) Here begins the Ch. version of this chapter.

[55]) *Asaṃkhyeya kalpa*. Four such aeons form a *mahākalpa*. For the numeral determination of an *asaṃkhyeya* see: Obermiller, *Bu-ston* I, p. 120 ff. and AK III, 188–190, IV, 224.

Ch. distinguishes the technical term *asaṃkhyeya (a-seng-chih)* from the *asaṃkhyeya* which precedes and means simply „incalculable" *(u shu)*.

[56]) *Abhāvasamudgata* = T. *Dṅos-po-med-pa-las-byuṅ-ba* = Ch. *Wu-so-yu-ch'i*.

[57]) Ch. „filled up completely" *(pien man)*.

[58]) *paraṃparayā*. Ch. om.

[59]) *vanaspatibhyaḥ* T. and. Ch. translate „from forests", relying probably upon the reading *vanaprasthebyaḥ* or simply *vanebhyaḥ*.

and from every summit of the mountains [60]), and as many as there were sound-manifestations [61]) in that world, the words announcing the „Birth of Non-existence" echoed by them all.

12) O Kumāra, at that very time, when the Lord, the Tathāgata, the Arhat, the Fully Enlightened One „Born of Non-existence" tought, there lived a prince, handsome, gracious and comely, Mahākaruṇācintin by name.

13) Now, o Kumāra, the prince Mahākaruṇācintin came to the presence of the Lord, the Tathāgata, the Arhat, the Fully Enlightened One „Born of Non-existence", inclined his head to the feet of the Lord, walked round him three times and stood aside.

14) Then, o Kumāra, the Lord, the Tathāgata, the Fully Enlightened One „Born of Non-existence" discerning the wish of the prince Mahākaruṇācintin tought him this *samādhi* [62]).

15) The prince, having heard of this *samādhi*, became satisfied and serene in spirit, shaved off hair and beard, dressed himself in yellow robes and with true faith left his home for the homeless state, Having been ordained, he learnt this *samādhi* [63]), by mastering it.

---

[60]) Ch. om.

[61]) *śabdaprajñapti* = *sgrar btags-pa* (Ch. om.). The stanzas 24, 25 of the VIIIth chapter which are a versified paraphrase of the present §, are quoted twice in the Pr.: pp. 278 (cf. the foot-notes 72 and 77) and 367_{13}. In the latter case the context of the Pr. explains the meaning of this place. There, a longer passage from the *Tathāgataguhyasūtra* is quoted (Pr. 366) according to which the Tathāgata beginning from the night of the *bodhi* till the night of the *parinirvāṇa* has not uttered any sound, and his teaching was magically preached by all the objects of the Universe. Then follows:

yathā yantrakṛtaṃ tūryaṃ vādyate pavaneritaṃ
na câtra vādakaḥ kaścin niścaranty atha ca svaraḥ
evaṃ pūrvasuśuddhatvāt sarvasattvāśayeritā
vāg niścarati buddhasya na câsyâstîha kalpanā

Cf. also the S. 284 (quoted from the *Dharmasaṃgītisūtra*): *yadi buddhā na bhavanti gaganatalād dharmaśabdo niścarati kuḍma-vṛkṣebhyaś ca.*

This is the well known Docetism of the Mahāyāna Buddhism. Cf. De la Vallée Poussin, *Opinions*, pp. 253—254, 259, *Ausgewählte Kapitel* p. 79, f.-note 55, and, in the *Samādhirājasūtra*, XIX, 23, 25 and the foot-note 129. The Brahmins, especially the Mīmāṃsakas, derided this conception, cf. JRAS, 1902, p. 374, f-note 1, and *Tattvasaṃgraha*, Gaekwad ed. kārikā 3241.

[62]) Ch. *shuo shih i ch'ieh chu fa t'i hsing p'ing teng wu hsi lun san mei* = *imaṃ sarva-dharma-svabhāva-samatā-vipañcitaṃ samādhiṃ deśayāmāsa*, cf. the f-notes 92,93.

[63]) Cf. the p. 21 and the f-note 20.

bearing it in mind [64]), reading [65]) it and applying himself to meditation [66]).

16) Owing to this store of merits, he was not reborn in the purgatory in a miserable state for 200 millions of aeons, propitiated [67]) 200 millions of Buddhas, and heard the teaching of this *samādhi* from all those Tathāgatas. Having heard it, he learnt it by mastering it, bearing it in mind, reading it, reciting [68]) it, practising concentration free from troubles [69]), repeating it and applying himself to meditation.

17) And owing to this store of former merits, he attained the Supreme Enlightenment after 200 millions of aeons, and appeared on earth as the Tathāgata, the Arhat, the Fully Enlightened One, Endowed with Wisdom and Virtue, the Sugata, the Knower of the World, the Supreme Guide of men who have to be restrained, the Teacher of gods and men, the Buddha and Lord, Suvicintitārtha by name [70]).

---

[64]) In T. the order of words is somewhat different, *kun-chub-par-byas-nas* (= *paryavāpya*) occurring in the fourth place.

[65]) This accessory meaning of *vācayati* is attested by T. *bklags* „to read" and by the Ch. *tu* „idem".

[66]) *bhavanāyogam anuyukto vyahārṣīt*, literally „was applying himself to application to meditation". Cf. the Pali formula *bhavanāyogam anuyutto* (Vibhaṅga 244).

This entire passage is usually not exactly rendered in Ch. Here *bhavanāyogam anuyukto* is omitted, but the translation of *parebhyo vistareṇa saṃprakāśayitvā* (cf. the f-note 155) is added.

[67]) *ārāgayāmāsa* = T. *mñes-par-byas-te*. Ch. „in every aeon he met (*chih*) 200000 Buddhas". The rest of the § is omitted in Ch.

[68]) *pravarttita* „to display, to drive, etc." T. *bton-to* (in other passages e.g. XXII, 8 *rab-tu-ldon-pa*) means „to recite". In Ch. *sung* would correspond to it.

[69]) AK I, 8 defines all the *sāsrava-skandhas* as *saraṇa*, cf. Museon, 1914, p. 35.

[70]) The readings of the Mss. as well as the versions of this § differ. In Ch. we find: „After 20 (sic) aeons he became a Buddha and appeared on earth as the Tathāgata etc. (epithets as in the Ms. C.).. Suvicintitārtha (*shan-ssŭ-i*) by name". Here the Ch. translation of the VIII th chpt. is finished. T. translates „And owing to this store of merits (om. „former") he attained the Supreme Enlightenment after 20 (sic) aeons and appeared on earth as the Tathāgata, the Arhat, the Fully Enlightened One, Suvicintitārtha (*don-legs-par-bsams-pa*) by name." The list of epithets is here shorter, like in the Mss. ABD.

18) Having brought to maturity innumerable and incalculable beings, and having saved innumerable beings [71]), he met the complete extinction like fire after exhaustion of fuel.

19) From this story, o Kumāra, let it be learnt by Thee how useful this *samādhi* is for the Bodhisattva-Mahāsattvas to attain the full knowledge of the Buddha".

20) Then the Lord, at that hour once again explained to the princely Candraprabha in detail, by reciting the verses, this chapter concerning the ancient times:

21) „I remember [72]), formerly, in the days of yore [73]), an inconceivable [number] of aeons ago, there appeared the Highest of men, the Great Sage, the Saviour of the World [74]). „Born of non-existence" was his name.

22) As soon as he was born, he proclamed, risen [75]) to the skies, the non-existence of all the *dharmas*. And having assumed a name in conformity with it, he instructed the entire Universe with this word.

23) And all the gods uttered these words: „That is certainly the Victorious One called „Non-existence", the Leader who, as soon as he was born, took seven steps and who proclaims the non-existence of the *dharmas* [76]).

---

[71]) *satvānām artham kṛtva*, literally „having fulfilled the task of the beings". It means the *pariṇāmana*. The Bodhisattva saves beings by the power of his own merits.

[72]) The stanzas 21—25 are quoted in Pr. p. 277—278 *(Ausgewählte Kapitel*, p. 78—79). The stanzas 24, 25 are quoted once again ibid. p. 367.

[73]) De la Vallée Poussin corrects: (Pr. p. 277_6) *atīta adhvani* which may be a specific sandhi of *atīte adhvani*. But *atītam adhvaní* is usual in Buddhist texts, cf. e. g. *Mahāvastu* (passim, side by side with *atītam adhvane*) and is doubtlessly produced by a confusion of two expressions: loc. temp. *atīte 'dhvani* and acc. temp. *atītam adhvanam*. The latter was felt as a single word *atītam-adhvanam* which had a regular declension.

[74]) *lokārthakara*, cf. the f.-note 71. We find in T. (as well as in the Tibetan translation of Pr.) *gziṅs-kyi don mdzad-pa*. De la Vallée Poussin (Pr. p. 277, foot-note 4) supposes, that the translator has read *kola* (=„canoe"= *gziṅs*) instead of *loka*.

[75]) Note the form *sthihitvā*, a gerund based on the Prakritic present stem *sthihate* (see F. Edgerton, *Gerunds in Buddhist Hybrid Sanskṛt*, Language, 13, Nr 2, 1937, pp. 114, 109, 117, Cf. the cf. note 147), T. in both xylographs: *rab-'du-gnas* which evidently must be corrected into *rab-tu-gnas=prasthitvā*.

[76]) T. *rgyal-bas chos-rnams dṅos-po-med-par bśad* corresponds to the reading preserved in Pr. (p. 278, f.-note 1) *abhāvu dharmāṇa... prakāśayi [jino]*.

24) And when this Sage, the Revealer of the essence of *dharmas* will become Buddha and King of Truth, then this utterance about the non-existent *dharmas* will resound in grass, trees, bushes, herbs, rocks and mountains".

25) And as many as there were sounds [77]) in that [78]) world, so manyfold [79]) was the utterance of this Tathāgata [80]), Leader of the World, [proclaiming] [81]): „All, indeed, is non existent, nothing is existent!"

26) At that time, there lived a prince, handsome, gracious [82]) and comely, Karuṇāvicintin [83]) by name, who came to the presence of the Victorious One,

27) worshipped the feet of the Supreme Sage, walked round him with veneration and sat down in order to listen with a serene spirit to the Supreme and Immaculate Truth.

28) And the Victorious and Wise One [84]), discerning his wish, revealed to him this *samādhi*. The Prince having heard

---

[77]) *śabda* which corresponds to *śabdaprajñapti* of the § 11. Cf. the foot-note 61.

[78]) *tahi* loc. of *ta-* or rather an adverbial formation like the Pali *tahiṃ*. Cf. *ekahi* (foot-note 110).

[79]) The forms *yāvanti śabdās... tāvantu svaru* offer some difficulties of interpretation, all the more because the Mss. differ. I adopt the reading of the second quotation in Pr. (p. 367_{16}; the first quotation on the p. 278_{11} has *tāvanti*) correcting only *tāvattu* into *tāvantu*, the groups *tt* and *nt* being almost identical in the Nepalese writing. C supplies a similar reading. *tāvantu* is to be interpreted as the transition of *tāvant* to the vowel declension, and may be a nomin. sing. like Pali *tāvanto* or Prakrit *mahantŏ kkhu*. An analogous interpretation may account for the form *yāvanti* from *yāvante* which can be considered as the nomin. plur. masc. analogous to the forms like *sarvi=sarve*. But a nomin. plur. *yāvante* not being found in any Middle Indian tongue, this interpretation wants proofs, and another explanation proposed to me by Prof. Jules Bloch seems more probable. He is inclined to see in the group *yāvanti śabdāḥ* a fact of syntactical evolution noticeable especially in the Numerals, which can occur in neuter plural before the Nouns of whatever gender, e. g. *trīṇi śabdāḥ*.

[80]) T. om.

[81]) I adopt the interpretation of T. which shows by the particle *źes* that *sarve hy abhāva* etc. are „oratio recta". In the somewhat awkward composition of the stanza these words depend on *yāvanti śabdāḥ* and not on *Tathāgatasya svaru*, but the corresponding passage in prose prooves that this utterance was first attributed to the Tathāgata and later to the World.

[82]) *prāsādiku* om. in T.

[83]) The name differs a little from the form of the prose story.

[84]) *dhīra*. T. *dpa'-bo* = *vīra*.

of this immaculate *samādhi*, embraced the religion of the greatest Conqueror immediately.

29) And having been ordained he bore this *samādhi* in mind, read it, mastered it, and for tull 200 millions of aeons never was he reborn [85]) in a miserable state.

30) By this meritorious deed he propitiated 200 millions of Buddhas and in the presence of all those Victorious Ones he practised this best and holy *samādhi*.

31) Afterwards he appeared on earth as the Buddha Suvicintitārtha by name, and having saved many millions of beings, became wholly extinct like a flame" [86]).

XIX.

1) Then the Lord spoke anew to the princely Candraprabha [87]): „Therefore, o Kumāra, the Bodhisattva-Mahāsattva who wishes not to be alarmed, frightened or terrified on hearing the immeasurable and

---

85) I preserve the reading of the Mss. ABD *jagmur* only changing the inappropriate plural into singular. C however gives *garccha* (?) which reminds the reading *gacchi* of the BTS edition. Would it be a peculiar Aorist?

86) K., at the end, adds a stanza:

dṅos-med-las-byuṅ-ṅo-bo-ñid
dṅos-po'i ṅo-bo-rnam-bsgoms-pas
bsgoms-pa'i stobs-kyis byuṅ gyur-pa
saṅs-rgyas dṅos-med-las-byuṅ dṅos

which, in the original, must have been a play of words (a frequent use of the group *bhāva*).

I give a literal rendering, trying to come near the probable śloka-rhythm of the original as for the three quarters at least (a, c, d):

abhāvodgatasvabhāvo bhāva-svabhāva-vibhāvanāt (?)
bhāvanā-balasaṃbhūto buddho 'bhāvasamudgato

„Having the essence born of non-existence (as there is no essence of existence) and owing to the power of meditation, a Buddha 'Born of Non-existence' was born".

Cf. a similar pun in the *Guhyasamāja Tantra* (Gaekwad's Or. Series, vol. LIII, p. 11):

abhāve bhāvanābhāvo bhāvanā naiva bhāvanā
iti bhāvo na bhāvaḥ syād bhāvanā nopalabhyate

(cf. the emendation of G. Tucci, *Mel. Chin. Bouddh.* III, p. 352, which however offers metrical difficulties).

87) Ch. om. this introductory formula.

inconceivable words [88]) of the merits [89]), advantages [90]) and achievements [91]) resulting from the *samādhi* which is explained [92]) as the equality of all the *dharmas* in their essence [93]), — [that Bodhisattva] should be expert in teaching the inconceivable *dharmas* of the Buddha,

2) should have faith in the inconceivable *dharmas* of the Buddha, be expert in questioning about the inconceivable *dharmas* of the Buddha and, on hearing of the inconceivable *dharmas* of the Buddha, he should not be alarmed, frightened or terrified" [94]).

3) At this the princely Candraprabha holding forth clasped hands spoke thus to the Lord: „How can a Bodhisattva-Mahāsattva, o Lord, be expert in teaching the inconceivable *dharmas* of the Buddha, have faith in the inconceivable *dharmas* of the Buddha, be expert in questioning etc. [95])... and how, on hearing of the inconceivable

---

[88]) The Mss. give this frequently occuring expression in very discrepant readings. In the § 1, A and D have *imān sarvadh⁰... vipañcitāyāḥ* (sic) *samādher acintyān aprameyāṃ gunānuś... padān*. The readings of B and C differ only in *imāni* and *⁰padā*. In the § 8, however, all the Mss. have *imāṃ s⁰... vipañcitāṃ samādher aprameyāṃ guṇā⁰... ⁰padāṃ*. If *padā* (nomin. plur neutr.) is possible, the masculine of *imāṃ... aprameyāṃ... padāṃ* is rather surprising, especially in prose passages which contain a rather regular Sanskrit. Thus it seems that both the feminine of *samādhi* and the masculine of *pada* should be explained as a fault of the scribe. Relying upon the passages (§§ 5, 14) where *vipañcitāt samādher* and (§ 9) *imāni... padāni* are found, I have corrected the text in all the other cases in the same way.

[89]) *guṇa=yon-tan*: 14 merits acquired during the meditative training. They are enumerated in the *Abhisamayālaṃkara-āloka;* cf. *The Doctrine of Pr. P.* pp. 78,88.

[90]) *ānuśaṃsa = phan-yon* (K. translates *rjes-su-bsṅags-pa* which is a wrong etymologisation), cf. e. g. Kern, translation of the *Saddharmapuṇḍarīka*, chapter XVIII; E. Obermiller, *The Sublime Science*, Acta Orientalia IX, p. 176.

[91]) *nirhāra = (b)sgrub-pa* (cf. *The Doctrine of Pr. P.* pp. 43, 75). This word is not translated in the §§ 1 (where *padāni* is missing too) and 8 of T.

[92]) *vipañcita = rnam-par-spros-pa*, cf. the Introduction, p. 22. The Ch. translation *wu hsi* is wrong and corresponds to *niṣprapañca*. *vipañcita* is rendered in the *Mahāvyutpatti* as *yen shuo* or *yu hsi shuo*.

[93]) *sarvadharmasamatā* „the equality of all the dharmas", the subject of the principal *samādhi* of the *Samādhirājasūtra*, see the Introduction p. 21 In Ch. the term is missing in this passage, but it occurs elsewhere, cf. the foot-note 62.

[94]) In Ch. the §§ 1, 2 are more laconic: „Therefore, o Kumāra, the Bodhisattva-Mahāsattva who strives for that *samādhi* should be an expert knower of the inconceivable dharmas *tought by the Buddhas*, should question about the inconceivable dharmas of the Buddha, should have faith in the inconceivable dharmas, etc. (the rest of the paragraph as in the original text).

[95]) T. om. the expression *acintyabuddhadharmaparyeṣaṇakuśala* here and in the § 4.

dharmas of the Buddha, can he not be alarmed, frightened or terrified"[96])?

4) At this the Lord spoke thus to the princely Candraprabha: „O Kumāra, the Bodhisattva-Mahāsattva who will hear of this *samādhi* explained as the equality of all the *dharmas* in their essence, and who will learn it, bear it in mind, read and master it, recite it, practise concentration free from troubles, and who will repeat this *samādhi* and explain it in detail to others[97]), that Bodhisattva-Mahāsattva will be expert in teaching the inconceivable *dharmas* of the Buddha, will have faith, etc.... ...and on hearing of the inconceivable *dharmas* of the Buddha, will not be alarmed, frightened or terrified".

5) And when the Lord had explained to the princely Candraprabha the words of the immeasurable merits, advantages and achievements resulting from the *samādhi* explained as the equality of all the *dharmas* in their essence, and when the princely Candraprabha had heard these inconceivable words of the merits etc..., then he attained this „King of *samādhis*" explained as the equality of all the *dharmas* in their essence.

6) And the immeasurable and innumerable Bodhisattva-Mahāsattvas attained the Great Knowledge and within the incalculable number of beings there arose the thought directed to the Great Knowledge and within the incalculable number of beings there arose the thought directed to the Great Compassion. And this Universe containing 3 thousand thousands of worlds shook[98]), moved, trembled tossed, roared and thundered, in six ways, viz.:

---

[96]) Ch. translates the § 3 as follows: „Then the princely Candraprabha spoke thus to the Buddha: ,O Lord, how should a Bodhisattva be an expert knower of the inconceivable dharmas of the Buddha, how will he inquire of the inconceivable dharmas of the Buddha, how will he have faith in the purity (sic: *shen hsin ts'ing tsing*) with regard to the inconceivable dharmas of the Buddha, and, on hearing of the inconceivable dharmas of the Buddha, how will he not be alarmed, frightened or terrified?"

After these words the translation of the § 11 begins immediately. Here evidently we have a gap, as is prooved by the lack of answer to the questions of Candraprabha.

As for the strange rendering of *acintyabuddhadharmâdhimukta*, especially compared with the preceding paragraph, *ts'ing tsing* seems to be a gloss. It is not unlikely that, in the original text, a gloss *śraddha* was added to *adhimukta* and that the Chinese translator has read it wrongly as *śuddha* = *ts'ing tsing*.

[97]) See VIII, 16, foot-note 66.

[98]) I refrain here from translating into English the threefold synonyms of every verb.

7) the eastern part sinks while the southern rises; the southern part sinks while the northern rises; the ends [of the world] sink while its middle rises; the ends rise while the middle sinks.

8) An immeasurable effulgence appeared on earth, a huge shower of heavenly perfumes fell, and all the gods and semigods, as many as there were of them, flew through the sky, assembled and sat together to listen to the Truth; having heard the immeasurable words of the merits, advantages and achievements resulting from the *samādhi* explained as the equality of all the *dharmas* in their essence, all those gods and semigods were pleased, delighted, enraptured, rejoiced, very satisfied, and they roared and ejaculated: „ha, ha, kilikila!"

9) They showered huge rains of multifarious kinds of heavenly flowers, and played on myriads of cymbals. And in one voice they uttered the following words: „It is indeed a great gain to us, that we have heard directly from the Lord those words of the immeasurable merits, advantages and achievements!

10) O Lord, we who are assembled here, should also like to attain such a *samādhi* explained as the equality of all the *dharmas* in their essence, as it was attained by the noble Bodhisattva-Mahāsattva Candraprabha!"

11) At that time, when the Lord tought the Truth on the Hill of „Vulture's-Peak", in an assembly great as the ocean, a *gandharva*, Pañcaśikha [99]) by name, flew down from the sky with 500 cymbals and stood before the Lord to worship him. [100]).

[99]) *Pañcaśikha* = T. *gtsug-phud-lṅa-can* = Ch. *pan-che-shih-ch'i* — one of the heavenly musicians, the attendant and messenger of Śakra (cf. e. g. *Sakkapañha-sutta*. Dīgh. Nik. II, 264—265, 269 etc.). Mlle M. Lalou points out („*Iconographie des étoffes peintes paṭa dans le Mañjuśri-mūlakalpa*" Buddhica VI, Paris, 1930, pp. 66—70, the analogy between that mythological personage and the Bodhisattva Mañjuśrī. One often represents Pañcaśikha as the emanation of the Brahma Sanatkumāra, a form of the eternally young Brahma. Manjuśri is always represented as a young royal prince (*kumārabhūta*). Mlle Lalou holds both divinities for having the same mythological source: the belief in an eternally young god.

The principal interlocutor of Buddha in our text, the Bodhisattva Candraprabha (in the *Mañjuśrīmūlakalpa* placed immediately after Mañjuśri, cf. M. Lalou, op. cit. p. 8) bears the same surname *kumārabhūta* (cf. M. Lalou, ibid. p. 32). In the light of the above facts, may the connection of Candraprabha and Pañcaśikha be not accidental?

[100]) Beginning from the § 11 we find a rather exact Ch. translation. Only instead of „with 500 cymbals" there is „with the 500 *gandharvas* of the common origin holding different musical instruments". Cf. the foot-note 104.

12) And it occurred to the *gandharva* Pañcaśikha: „Let me [101]) give a concert to worship the Supreme God, the Tathāgata, the Arhat, the Fully Enlightened One, just as I play in the Heavenly Hall[102]) before the assembly of gods to worship the Thirty Three and their ruler Śakra! [103])".

13) And while those 500 cymbals produced one concordant sound [104]), the *gandharva* Pañcaśikha himself played on the lute having a *vaiḍūrya*-handle [105]), before the Lord.

14) And it occurred to the Lord: „Let me perform such a magic [106]) that the princely Candraprabha could acquire the skill to understand the inconceivable *dharmas* of the Buddha, and owing to which he would not deviate from this *samādhi* explained as the

---

[101]) *yaṃ nv' aham* evidently corresponds to the Pali formula *yaṃ nūn' âhaṃ* „let me". Note the use of *nu* instead of *nūnam*.

[102]) *Sudharmā* = T. *chos-bzaṅ*. Ch. om.

[103]) Ch.: *Śakra (ti shih) Kauśika (chiao-shih-chia)*.

[104]) Ch.: „Then the *gandharva* Pañcaśikha and 500 other *gandharvas*, every one of them struck the *vaiḍūrya*-lutes producing marvellous music". But the Sanskrit text, where the cymbals produce sounds of themselves, corresponds better to the Docetic ideas of the *Samādhirājasūtra*. Cf. also the foot-note 108.

[105]) *vaiḍūryadaṇḍā vīnā*, a magical lute belonging first to Māra from whom it was taken away by Śakra and given to Pañcaśikha (cf. *Paramatthajotikā*, II, p. 393). This form of the word occurs in the Sanskrit Buddhist Texts, cf. e. g. *Avadānaśataka*, Bibl. Buddh. III, vol. I, p. 9. In Pali, however, another form *beluvapaṇḍuvīnā* is met with, which means „yellow lute made of Vilva wood". But this interpretation is not quite certain, since we find in Pali texts also *veḷuvadaṇḍavīnā* (cf. the Ms. K of the Commentary to the Dhammapada, I, p. 433) where *veluva* may mean „made of cane", cf. the Sanskrit *vaiṇava*. In that case rather a kind of flute was meant. Besides, both *beluva* and *veluva* may represent the difformed *vaiḍūrya*. At any rate this first component of the word offered no difficulty to the translators; the doubt arose with the second term *daṇḍa*= „handle" (cf. *Saṃyutta-Nikāya*, IV, p. 196). T. translates *pi-waṇ-gi khog-pa baidu-rya-byas-pa* = „the frame of the lute made of *vaiḍūrya*". This *khog-pa* would correspond rather to the part of the lute called *upaveṇa* (see the above quoted passage of *Saṃyutta-Nikāya* where all the parts of a *vīnā* are enumerated, and „*The Book of Kindred Sayings*", P. T. S., translation series N 14, vol. IV, p. 129, foot-note 5). Ch. om. this word and translates simply „*vaiḍūrya* lute" *(liu li ts'in)*.

[106]) *ṛddhyabhisaṃskāra*, in Ch. translated: *vikrīḍitarddhi* (*yu hsi shen li*) *anabhisaṃskāra (sic! wu tso)*.

equality of all the *dharmas* in their essence. Let me teach the *gandharva* Pañcaśikha the skill to sing and play on strings! [107])"

15) And the Lord performed such a magic, that out of those 500 cymbals well harmonized and producing concordant sounds [108]) there came a voice having an inconceivable meaning concerning the Absolute. And so, owing to the magical power of the Buddha there resounded the following verses giving the understanding of the inconceivable *dharmas* of the Buddha [109]):

16) „On the point of a single [110]) hair there are as many Buddhas as there are grains of sand on the bank [111]) of the Ganges [112]).

---

[107]) Ch.: „...that the princely Candraprabha could attain the stability of a concentrated mind (*i hsin chu* = *ekāgracittasthiti)* within the inconceivable dharmas of the Buddha, and moreover let me make the instruments of Pañcaśikha and other *gandharvas* produce sounds and let me display an uncommon miracle!"

[108]) Ch. „the *gandharvas* playing independently of their will".

[109]) Cf. the similar situation in the above quoted (f.-note 105) passage of the *Avadānaśataka*.

[110]) *ekahi*, locative of *eka* formed probably analogically to *tahi*.

[111]) T. and Ch. „in the river Ganges".

[112]) The following stanzas must, according to the wish of the Tathāgata (§ 14), make it easy for Candraprabha to understand the thesis of the equality of all the dharmas (cf. also the § 34). This thesis is illustrated in the stanzas 16—24 by the old Buddhist mythological conception, according to which the entire Universe is placed on the point of a hair of the Buddha. We find this conception frequently in the Buddhist texts, e. g. in the *Avataṃsaka* (transl. of D. T. Suzuki, EB, I, 2, p. 152):

„All the Buddhalands and all the Buddhas themselves are manifested in my own being, freely and without hindrance, and even at the point of a single hair a Buddhaland is perceived".

Suzuki calles this conception „intermutuality"; it means that „each object is not only itself, but every other object and that all things are mutually conditioned". It is possible, because according to the *Avataṃsaka* the Absolute is identical with the consciousness immanent in every being (*sarvasattvacitta*, cf. St. Schayer, *Das mahāyānistische Absolutum*, OLZ, 1935, col. 406).

In our text this hair containing the entire Universe seems to represent that consciousness, though it is not stated expressly. Such is at least the interpretation of K.: *rmi-lam-gyi naṅ-du lha-la-sogs-pa'i bde-ba ñams-su myoṅ-ba daṅ / bźon-pa sna-tshogs daṅ / gźal-yas khaṅ-la-sogs-pa mthoṅ yaṅ khyim der de-dag gźugs-pa yaṅ ma-yín de-nas phyir byuṅ-ba yaṅ med-do // de-bźin-du raṅ-gi sems tsam-las tha-mi-dad-pa'i dṅos-po don-gyis stoṅ-pa dmigs-su med-pa / rmi-lam-du snaṅ-ba ltar ma-rig-pa'i bag-chags-kyis bsgos-pa'i sems-ñid phyin-ci-log-tu dmyal-ba-la-sogs-par rab-tu-snaṅ-ṅo // byaṅ-chub-kyi sems-daṅ / pha-rol-tu-phyin-pa'i bag-chags-kyis bsgos-pa'i sems-la ni de-bźin-gśegs-pa-la-sogs-par snaṅ-bar 'gyur-ro źes*

There are as many spheres of the Victorious Ones which are all different [113]) and incommensurable [114]).

17) On the point of a hair there are beings of all the five regions: the damned of the purgatory, the brute creation, inhabitants of the world of Yama, gods and men. Yet, are they neither mixed [115]), nor squeezed [116]).

18) In this space [117]) there are oceans, lakes, all the rivers, springs and ponds. Yet they are neither mixed nor squeezed. So inconceivable are the *dharmas* of the Victorius Ones.

---

bya'o // skra gcig khyon-la-ste / spu'i khuṅ-bur saṅs-rgyas maṅ-por gaṅ-gā'i kluṅ-gi bye-ma'i graṅs daṅ mñam-par rab-tu snaṅ-ṅo = „One enjoys in the dream divine pleasures and one sees different carriages, immense palaces etc. But, as they are not in this place, [one cannot tell that] they actually exist. Yet, one does not in this way imagine the [absolute] emptiness, because we admit that the reality is not different from the 'mind alone'. Like in dreams, those whose mind is determined by the stamp *(bag-chags* = *vāsana)* of ignorance, being deceived, see hells, etc.; and those whose mind is determined by the stamp of the Thought of Enlightenment and the Highest Perfection *(pāramitā)*, see the Tathāgata, etc. Therefore it seems that 'on the point of a single hair' i. e. in one pore of the hair there are as many Buddhas, as there are grains of sand in the river Ganges." Thus all the dharmas are equal, because they are contained in the same point of a hair, i. e. are created by the same mind. Cf. the stanzas 26, 27 which develope the same idea as K.

In the subsequent stanzas the interpretation of the thesis *sarvadharmasamatā* is not expressly idealistic and consists rather in gathering of contrasts in order to point out their identity, or, more frequently in order to recommend the general Buddhist *madhyamā pratipad* „the avoiding of both extremities" (cf. the §§ 28, 32, 33, 34).

[113]) *vilakṣaṇa* = T. *mtshan-ñid-mi-'dra*. T. shows that „spheres having unequal marks" are meant. Ch. *wu hsiang* = *alakṣaṇa*.

[114]) *visabhāga* = *skal-mi-mñam* „incommensurable, belonging to different classes", cf. e. g. Pr. p. 321: *visabhāga* = *bhinnajātiyā*. Ch. here too, is inexact: *t'i k'ung* corresponds rather to *niḥsvabhavā* which could, besides, be a false reading for *visabhāga*. Cf. the foot-note 198.

[115]) Literally: „there is no commingling *(na saṃkara* = *'dres-pa-med;* Ch. *ts'ing liang* „coolness, serenity" = *śītibhāva*) and no pressure".

[116]) *upīḍa*, a dialectical f rm derived from **opīḍa* < *avapīḍa* „pressing down". A derivation from *utpīḍa* „pressing out" (simplification of the geminate *upīḍa* < **uppīḍa* < *utpīḍa*) might be possible, but is less likely, since such forms in our text generally maintain the original spelling (cf. *utpādo* pronounced *upādo* XIX, 22a). Ch. *pien tse* „pressed, strait, narrow". T. *gnod-par-'gyur-ba* „oppressed, hurt, damaged".

[117]) Ch. translates here and in a number of subsequent stanzas: „in the space of a hair".

19) In this space there are also many mountains: Cakravāḍa, Meru, Sumeru, Mucilinda, the Great Mucilinda, Vindhya, Gṛdhrakūṭa and Himalaya [118]).

20) In this space there are also terrible hells: the Hot Hell the Very Hot Hell, etc. [119]); those who are reborn in these hells suffer pains.

21) In this space there are also charming [120]) divine palaces, 12 *yojanas* [121]) long, where many thousand gods [122]) enjoy pleasures and heavenly bliss.

22) In this space there appear the Buddhas [123]) and there shines the teaching of the Knowers of the World. It is invisible to one deprived of knowledge or to one whose conduct [124]) is not perfectly pure.

---

[118]) Ch. om. these (not mythical) mountains and repeats instead the last line of the stanza 18: „So inconceivable are the dharmas of the Buddha".— Prof. Helmer Smith points out that the pāda *b* (possibly also *d*) of this stanza agrees with the common *Dodhaka* in the number of syllabic instances, viz. 6 + 4 + 4 + 2 *mora* : ⏓ ⏑⏑ ⏑⏑ ⏓ | ⏓ — | ⏑⏑ — | —; „this analysis has been applied in the *Copenhagen Pali Dictionary* (s. vv. *apilapati, aparājitasamgha apāyabhūmi)* to ‚irregular' verses as SN, I, 29[27] —31[4] and ib. 26[23] —27[11] = DN, II, 254[6] —255[5] (regulated as '*proto-Svāgatā*' in the Sanskrit diorthosis, *Preuss. Turfan Expedition, Kl. Sanskrit-Texte*, ed. Waldschmidt, p. 161, note 2); before ending in the *Caupāī* of the Hindi Epic this popular pāda was differenciated by Apabhraṃśa writers into *Adilā* and *Pādākulaka*, so ably described in L. Alsdorf's *Harivaṃśapurāṇa*, p. 191—192 (cf. Piṅgala IV, 47)".— As for the pāda *d*, *Vindhyâtha* is a late correction for *Vindhy'atha;* I read *Vindhy'atha Gṛdhrakūṭo Himavaṃś ca* where *ū* of *Gṛdhrakūṭa* remains metrically unexplained. Prof. Helmer Smith thinks that *atha* is spurious altogether, and prefers *Vindhya* (°*yu*) *Gṛdhrakūṭo Himavaṃś ca:* — ⏑ — ⏑ | — — | ⏑ ⏑ — | ⏓.

[119]) These are two of the hot hells. K. quotes one more: *dmyal-ba tsha-ba daṅ rab-tu-tsha-ba daṅ | thig-nag-la-sogs-pa-rnams* = „The hells: the 'Hot-Hell' *(tapana)*, the 'Very-Hot-Hell' *(pratapana)*, the 'Hell of the Black String' (*kāla-sūtra)* etc.". Ch. enumerates other categories of hells: the burning hells (*huo chiao jo*), the freezing hells (*han ping*) and the excrement hells (*fen shih)*.

[120]) In T. both xylographs give *dbyaṅs dga'-ba* which is incomprehensible. An emendation *dbyiṅs dga'-ba* „heavenly delightful" seems very probable.

[121]) Ch.: „16 *yojanas* (*shih liu hsün*)".

[122]) *marutāna* = T. *lha'i*= Ch. *t'ien*, cf. *Mahāvastu* 18, 68, *marū-narā* „gods and men", 15, 211 *marūgaṇā* „hosts of gods".

[123]) Literally: „is the appearing of the Buddhas". Ch. *fo ch'u shih* „the sphere of the appearing of the Buddhas".

[124]) Ch. *hsü i* „former deeds".

23) In this space one hears the words: „The *dharma* was dissolved and the Leader attained the Nirvāṇa [125])!" And in this space others hear: „The Leader still exists and teaches the Truth!"

24) In this space some think [126]) that life lasts for an inconceivable number of years [127]). But in this space also are heard the words: „One dies [128]) and does not live any longer".

25) And others think that they have seen the Tathāgata and worshipped the Buddha. But their mind is delighted only with its own imagination; [in reality] they neither worshipped [the Buddha], nor was he born [129]).

26) Just as a man sleeping in his house enjoys sensual pleasures [130]), but when awakening does not perceive these pleasures and realizes that it was but a dream,

27) so all that [131]) is seen, heard, thought and known, is all untrue like a dream. And he [alone] who practises this *samādhi* [132]) will realize the essence of the *dharmas*.

---

[125]) T.: „one hears the words of the Leader who dissolved the Dharma and attained the Nirvāṇa".

[126]) *keṣacid... saṃjñā* = T. *la-la-dag... sñam-'dzin* = „the idea of some people is that..."

[127]) *varṣa acintiya*. The ending *ă* of the acc. plur. masc. is rather seldom in the Buddhist Sanskrit, cf. however *Rāṣṭrapālaparipṛchā* 54, 17: *kalpān acintya*. It is a shortening analogous to the one which is produced in the ending of the gen. plur. *ānă* > *ānāṃ*. Ch: „their life is inexhaustible (*wu ch'iung chi*)".

[128]) *kālu karonti* = T. *'chi-ba'i dus byed-ciṅ*.

[129]) The T. translation corresponds to *mānasasamjñāgraheṇa* and replaces Tathāgata by Sugata. The stanzas 23 and 25 give a Docetic solution of two false alternatives: a) the Buddha has attained the Nirvāṇa, and b) the Buddha still exists and teaches. In reality he is never born nor does he strive for Nirvāṇa. Cf. *Aspects* p. 111.

[130]) *kāmaguṇeṣu* — five kinds of sensual pleasures corresponding to the five senses: Ch. translates „five pleasures (*wu yü*)".

[131]) This pāda is defective and may be corrected into *yat tatha dṛṣṭu* etc. see p. 46 the f.-note 18.

[132]) Note the strange form *samādhiya*. Could it be the gen sing. feminine? Cf. °*vipañcitāyāḥ samādher* XIX, I (f. -note 88). Or a gen. sing. masc. like the Prakritic *aggīo* gen. of *aggi*? Less likely is the suggestion that this expression is to be read *samādhipalābhi* = *samādhipralābhi* (*p* and *y* being very similar in the Nepalese writing).

28) Full happy [133]) are always those on earth to whom nothing is dear or hated [134]), and those who dwelling in forest-caves enjoy the ascetic's happiness,

29) and those who have no belongings or anything about which they may say: „it is mine"; they walk through this world lonely as a rhinoceros [135]), and wander like the wind in the sky.

30) Practised [136]) is the Path, and achieved the Knowledge that all the *dharmas* are void and unsubstantial. He who understands clearly those *dharmas* will acquire the infinite intelligence [137]).

31) Full happy, indeed, are those on earth whose mind does not cling to the world; their mind is always like the wind and they are free from attachment to what is dear or hated.

32) To live with the hated is suffering, to separate from what is dear is suffering too, but those who have abandoned both, are happy and have pleasure in the Truth.

33) He who having listened to good *dharma* is attracted [by it], is repulsed when listenig to bad *dharma*. Such a person errs afflicted by the intoxication of vanity and, being subject to pride, suffers pain [138]).

---

[133]) §§ 28, 29, 31, 32 are quoted in S. pp. 194_{12-15}, 195.

[134]) K.: *yul-rnams-la sdug-pa dan mi sdug-pa'i spobs-pa-dag ni mtha'-yas-gyur*=„He to whom among the objects (*viṣaya*) nothing is dear or hated, acquires the infinite intelligence". Cf. the § 30.

[135]) A usual comparison for a Pratyekabuddha, cf. *Sutta Nipāta* 6—12, *Mahāvastu* pp. 357—359, *Divyāvadāna* pp. 294, 582.

[136]) This stanza is quoted in Pr. 258_{1-5} (wrongly attributed to the *Upāliparipṛcchā*).

[137]) *pratibhāna*, properly speaking „promptitude of mind". Cf. T. *spobs* „self confidence" and Ch. *pien tsai* „ability in debate".

[138]) Ch.: „He who, having heard these words, has passion, within him anger should arise". The rest corresponds to the original text.

K.: *gaṅ-źig chos ni thos-nas chags-byed-ciṅ źes bya-ba-la / mya-ṅan-las-'das-pa daṅ / rjes-su-mthun-pa ni chos-ñid yin-no źes thos-nas rjes-su-chags-pa'i dbaṅ-gis mṅon-par-źen-no // chos-ma-yin-pa ni dmyal-ba-la-sogs-pa'i rgyu yin-no źes khoṅ-khro-ba skyed-par byed-do / chos daṅ chos-ma-yin-pa mñam-pa-ñid-du ma-rtogs-pas ṅa-rgyal daṅ rgyags-pa'i dbaṅ-gis sdug-bsṅal ñams-su-myoṅ-bar 'gyur /* = „He who, having heard that there exist dharmas corresponding to Nirvāṇa, is possessed by attachment,—or, having heard that there exist bad dharmas leading to the hells, feels anger, — such a man, not realizing the identity of the good and the bad dharma, is infatuated by vanity and will suffer pain".

34) Those who are grounded in the equality [of all the *dharmas*], who are neither arrogant nor cringing, and who are free [from attachment] to what is dear or hated, — are always delivered in spirit.

35) Those who are always grounded in the perfectly pure virtues and in the inconceivable [139]) concentrations, and who dwell in the peaceful forest-caves, are free from all doubts [140]).

36) But those fools who always depend on untruth and indulge in sensual pleasures like vultures clinging to carcass, are in the eternal power of Namuci".

37) And owing to this application of verses emanating from the sounds of the lute [141]) the princely Candraprabha acquired the skill to understand and interprete the profound *dharmas* of the Buddha [142]), and the *gandharva* Pañcaśikha attained the state of acceptance of Buddha's oral teaching [143]). And within the incalculable number of beings among gods and men there arose the thought of the Supreme Enlightenment, and innumerable beings were saved.

---

139) Ch. has *nirmālacitta (wu kou hsin)* instead of *acintya*.

140) Ch.: „They are free from the snares of doubt". K.: *de-dag ni tshul-khrims yoṅs-su-dag-pa daṅ / bzod-pa daṅ / brtson-'grus daṅ / bsam-gtan daṅ / śes-rab-la rab-tu-gnas-pa źes bya'o //* „By this are meant those who are grounded: 1) in the perfectly pure morality, [i. e. in virtues like] forbearance (*kṣānti*) and energy (*vīrya*), 2) in concentration (*dhyāna*) and 3) in knowledge (*prajñā*)." This is the well-known climax *śīla, samādhi, prajñā* on which is based the scheme of the *Visuddhimagga*. In the stanza XIX, 35, to the element *prajñā* corresponds the expression „free from doubts".

141) Ch.: „during the reciting of those verses".

142) Ch.: „Candraprabha attained the stability of the concentrated mind (*i hsin an chu*) and the skill to interprete (*yen shuo*) the sūtras.

143) *ghoṣānugā kṣānti*. D. T. Suzuki (*Studies in the Laṅkāvatārasūtra*, London, 1930, pp. 125—127), points out that the Pali meaning of *kṣānti* „patience, forbearance" does not ever suit the Mahāyāna texts where *kṣānti* often has the sense of a willing compliance or acceptance. See AK. VII, 1, 2: „...La patience (*kṣānti*) n'est pas exempte de doute puisqu'elle a pour fin de produire le savoir par l'expulsion du doute. Elle ne naît pas comme certitude (*niścaya*), mais comme „acquiescement" (*kṣamanarūpeṇa*)... Ces huit espèces de *kṣānti* sont „vues" (*darśana*), parce que, de leur nature, elles sont „d'examen" (*saṃtīrṇātmakatvāt*)". Cf. ibid. IV, p. 209: „Le possesseur de la *kṣānti*, quoique „sot" (*pṛthagjana*), est reputé „semblable à celui qui a vu des vérités (*dṛṣṭasatyakalpa*)".

There are different lists of *kṣāntis*. In the *Avataṃsakasūtra* (*Śikṣānanda*, chptr XXIX) ten kinds are enumerated. A more archaic list contains but 3 *kṣāntis* (*Sukhāvativyūha*, S. B. E. XLIX, p. 51, § 32): 1) *ghoṣānugā kṣānti*, 2) *anulo-*

XXII.

1) Then the Lord spoke anew to the princely Candraprabha: „Therefore, o Kumāra, a Bodhisattva-Mahāsattva who strives for this *samādhi* and wishes to attain the Supreme Enlightenment speedily, must not cling to the body [144]) and life".

2) „For what reason?" — „Because, o Kumāra, in consequence of the clinging to the body and life, the active dispositions of beings[145]) become unfavourable.

3) But for the Bodhisattva-Mahāsattvas who do not cling to the body and life, the Supreme Enlightenment is not hard to attain. And how much [easier] this *samādhi*! Therefore, o Kumāra, Thou shalt always meditate in the following manner: „I shall not cling to the body and life!" Since it is said:

---

mikī kṣānti and 3) *anutpattikadharmakṣānti.* The same three kinds are mentioned in the *Samādhirājasūtra* where a special chapter (VII, *Trikṣāntyavatāra*) is devoted to their description.

Suzuki, refering to *Avataṃsaka,* defines the *ghoṣānugā kṣānti* as: „to listen to the oral teaching of the Buddha, to accept it without fear or hesitation and to abide in it whole-heartedly". We meet a similar conception of the *ghoṣānugā kṣānti* in the aforesaid *Trikṣāntyavatāra,* as can be proved by the following quotations:

sa sarvasūtrāntanayeṣu kovidaḥ
subhāṣitasminn adhimuktva paṇḍitaḥ
anantajñānī sugatāna jñāne
prathamāya kṣāntiya ime viśeṣāḥ

. . . .

yat kiñci dharmaṃ śṛṇute subhāṣitaṃ
buddhāna co bhāṣitu tan na kāṃkṣati
adhimucyate sarvajināna dharmatāṃ
prathamāya kṣāntiya ime viśeṣāḥ

. . . .

nitārthā sūtrāntaviśeṣa janati
yathopadiṣṭāṃ sugatena śūnyatāṃ
yasmin punaḥ pudgalu śāntu jīno
neyārthatāṃ jānati sarvadhārmān.

[144]) T. makes the meaning of the Sanskrit *kāya* more precise: *lus* corresponds merely to the human physical body, while the Bodies of the Tathāgata are denoted by the honorific *sku.*

[145]) I am correcting the text according to T. The readings of the Mss. might arise from a confusion with the subsequent sentence. Ch. translates: „Those who cling to the body produce the unfavourable dharmas".

4) Fools that constantly [146]) clung to the foul and impermanent body, and who adhered to life in search of happiness, those fools ever commited [147]) sins.

5) But those who are free from attachment to the body and the unessential life, having destroyed the army [148]) of Māra, attained Enlightenment [149]) under the Bodhi-tree.

6) Those who on the contrary are attached to both: the unsubstantial and empty body and the powerless [150]) life resembling dreams, after death go to hells [151])".

---

146) Both the readings *'nitye* and *nitye* are possible. In the first case *'nitye* would be a definition of *kāyi*. It seems better to avoid the pleonastic *aśāśvati anitye* and to adopt *nitye* „always". Such is the T. translation, moreover, the reading *śāśvati* = *khor-mor* is adopted, so that T. is to be translated: „Fools that constantly and continually cling to the foul body..."

147) *pāpaṃ kurviṣu* = *sdig-pa byed. kurviṣu*, 3d pers. plur. of the sibilant Aorist is frequent in the Buddhist Sanskrit, cf. *Saddharmapuṇḍarīka* I, 11 *kurviṣu*, II, 82 *krīḍiṣu; Daśabhūmikasūtra* VI, 13 *prekṣiṣu*, VII, 1 *abhikiriṣu; Samādhirājasūtra*, chptr X (*Purapraveśa*) *vandiṣu*, etc. As for such Aorists based on thematic Present stems, cf. the Prakritic *vikuvviṃsu* (*Vivāhapannatti*, 214, 215) and F. Edgerton, *The Aorist in Buddhist Hybrid Sanskrit*, JAOS, 57, p. 20 and Language, 13, N 2, p. 114.

148) Note the syntax of °*camūnām*, gen. instead of acc.

149) The Mss. have *prabudhyiya*. If we accept this reading, then we get in this stanza only two Gerunds *nihanitvāna* and *prabudhyiya* and no „verbum finitum". Though such anacoluthe were possible, the emendation *prabudhyiṣu*, that Prof. J. Bloch and Prof. H. Smith propose to me, seems more likely. It would be a sibilant Aorist like *kurviṣu* of the preceding stanza and the construction of two stanzas would be analogous: *karitvāna* — *kurviṣu* : *nihanitvāna* — *prabudhyiṣu*. The confusion of final *ya* and *ṣu* is easy to explain graphically, cf. the stanza XXII, 4 where Mss. AD write *avalaṃbiṣa* for *avalaṃbiya*.

150) The strange form (*a*)*vaśye* is found also in the variant of this stanza quoted in S. (see the subsequent foot-note): *jīvite cañcale 'vaśye*. W. H D. Rouse (*Śiksha-samuccaya*, London, 1922, p. 20) translates: „life that must needs be unsteady". In our text, T. translates *zil-pa*: „[life resembling] the hoar-frost" which would correspond to the Sanskrit *avaśyāya* (masc.) or *avaśyā* (fem). A masc. *avaśya*, however, is not known, and the syntactical construction is embarassing, because this word should be connected with °*nibhe*, from which it is separated by *cali*. Perhaps Prof. H. Smith is right in thinking of an adj. *avaśya* „not dependent of one's will, unreliable"; however the Upaniṣadic use — *tasyendriyāny avaśyāni duraśvā iva sāratheḥ*, Kāṭh. 1, 3, 5 is a poor evidence.

In this stanza ends the XXII chpt of the T. version. In Ch. the stanzas 4—6 are not translated at all.

151) Cf. an interesting variant quoted in S. 18_{11-14} as coming from *Candrapradīpa:*

7) Then the Lord spoke anew to the princely Candraprabha: „Therefore, o Kumāra, a Bodhisattva-Mahāsattva who strives for this *samādhi* and wishes to attain the Supreme Enlightenment speedily, must not conceive the true nature of the Tathāgata in the aspect of the Material Body".—„For what reason?" — „Because the true nature [152]) of the Buddhas is their Absolute Body and not the Material Body.

8) Therefore, o Kumāra, a Bodhisattva-Mahāsattva who wishes to adore the Body of the Tathāgata, who wishes to know the Body of the Tathāgata, must learn this *samādhi* [153]), master it, bear it in mind, read it, recite it, teach it, learn it by heart, apply himself to meditation [154]) and explain this *samādhi* in detail to others [155]).

---

adhyavasitā ye bālāḥ kāye 'smin pūtike samyag
jīvite cañcale 'vaśye māyāsvapnanibhopame
atiraudrāṇi karmāṇi kṛtvā mohavaśānugāḥ
te yānti narakān ghorān mṛtyuyānagatâbuddhā.

This quotation is not yet found in the Mss. of the *Samādhirājasūtra*, and, on account of its rather regular Sanskrit which differs from the poetical vernacular of our text, it seems that the aforesaid verses are not a quotation, but a free paraphrase of the XXII, 4—6.

152) Literally: „the Buddhas are conditioned (*°prabhāvita)* by the Absolute Body". Ch. translates: „The Buddhas are connected *(she)* with the Absolute Body, not with the Material Body; the Buddhas manifest themselves *(hsien hsien = abhivyañj-)* as the Absolute Body, not as the Material Body". The T. *rab-tu-phye-ba* gives for *prabhāvita* the meaning „opened, manifesting itself", but in K. the term is rendered by *bsgos-pa* = „conditioned", and this seems to be the best translation. K.: *gzugs-kyi skus mṅon-par-rdzogs-par saṅs-rgyas-pa yin-la de'i phyir sku gaṅ-gis mṅon-par-saṅs-rgyas-pa de-ñid skur lta-bar-bya'o żes bya-ba'i the-tshom yoṅs-su-spoṅ-bar byed-pa-ste / chos-kyi skus bsgos-pa ni gzugs-kyi sku yin-la / chos-kyi sku ni gzugs-kyi skus bsgos-pa yaṅ ma-yin-te...* = „[One could think thus]: ‚since [the Buddha] attained the Supreme Enlightenment in the Material Body, he should be cognized in this Body in which he attained the Enlightenment'. But having rejected those doubts [one should think in the following manner]: ‚the Material Body is conditioned by the Absolute Body, but the Absolute Body is not conditioned by the Material Body..."

153) Cf. the foot-note 20.

154) Ch. translates *hsiu hsi* „to practise the *yoga*", T. „to meditate and apply oneself to meditation".

155) Ch. translates exactly: *t'a kuang shuo*, but this expression precedes *hsiu hsi*. The practice of the *samādhi* is necessary in order to know the Body of Buddha, because this *samādhi* is the essence of the Absolute Body. Cf. K. (on XXII, 13): *tiṅ-ṅe-'dzin-gyi ṅo-bo-ñid ni sku yin-pas tiṅ-ṅe-'dzin-gyi ṅo-bo gaṅ-gis mthoṅ-ba des de-bżin-gśegs-pa'i sku bsod-nams daṅ ye-śes-kyi tshogs-las ṅes-par-*

9) Now, o Kumāra, the Body of the Tathāgata should be defined[156]) as synonymous with the Intellect born of innumerable merits[157]), as born of *dharmas*, markless[158]), free from all marks, profound[159]), unknowable[160]), consisting of unknowable *dharmas*[161]), having a markless essence, deprived of all marks, motionless, unfixed[162]), having its essence identical with Space[163]), invisible, surpassing the range of vision — thus is the Absolute Body to be conceived.

---

byuṅ-ba mthoṅ-ba yin-no // = „Since the Body is the Essence of the *samādhi*, he who sees the Essence of the *samādhi*, sees also the Body of the Tathāgata born of the accumulation of merits and wisdom".

156) *nirdeśo* the syntactical meaning of which is not quite clear. Prof. J. Przyluski proposes the correction °*nirdeśyo*.

157) This passage is not clear. T. translates rather *śatapuṇyanirjāto buddhyekārthanirdeśo (nirdiṣṭo* or °*nirdeśyo*). Ch. *wu liang fu te chih so ch'u sheng ju lai shuo yü i i* means: *„born of immeasurable merits and tought by the Buddha as One single Object"*. The Ch. translator has read *Buddha* (*ju lai*) instead of *buddhi*.

158) Ch. om.

159) Ch., beginning from here, joins almost all the epithets in pairs signifying the relation between the two parts by means of the particles i_1 and *ku*, e. g. „free from all marks, because profound" etc.

160) *apramāṇa*. K.: *tshad-med-pa mṅon-sum daṅ / rjes-su-dpag-pa daṅ / luṅ-gi tshad-mas rtogs-par-byar-med-pa'i phyir-ro* // = „unknowable, because it cannot be cognized through the modes of cognition such as : perception (*pratyakṣa*), inference (*anumāna*) and sacred testimony (*āgama*)". These are the 3 sources of knowledge adopted by the Buddhists before the reform of *Dignāga* who rejected *āgama*. Ch. om. the epithet *apramāṇa*.

161) Ch. adds *wu fen ch'i* „homogeneous, undifferentiated (*anavayava, nirviśeṣa*)".

162) *apratiṣṭhita* = T. *mi-gnas-pa* = „unfixed (either in *saṃsāra* or in *nirvāṇa*) K.: *mi-gnas-pa'i mya-ṅan-'das-pa'i ṅo-bo-ñid-kyis thams-cad-du ṅes-par-gnas-pa-ñid* = „unfixed in the sense of the unfixed *nirvāṇa*. That means: omnipresent (and helping to attain salvation, *ṅes-par-gnas-pa* = *upasthita*). Cf. De la Vallée Poussin, *Siddhi*. p. 671: „L'Apratiṣṭhita Nirvāṇa = la Tathatā... n'est pas fixée dans le saṃsāra en raison de la science ou savoir (*jñāna*), ni non plus dans le nirvāṇa en raison de la pitié... Elle pourvoit au bonheur et au salut des êtres". Cf. J. Masuda, *Der Individualistische Idealismus der Yogācāra Schule*, p. 49 and the detailed description of the *apratiṣṭhita nirvāṇa* in Obermiller's, *Nirvāṇa according to the Tibetan Tradition*, IHQ, X, N 2, 1934, pp. 252-257. Ch. translates here *shan an chu* = *supratiṣṭhita*.

163) Ch. instead of this gives *wu yu erh wei i hsiang ku* = „*advaya*, because it has only one mark".

10) Inconceivable, surpassing the sphere of thought, not oscillating between bliss and suffering [164]), surpassing the illusory differenciation [165]), placeless [166]), surpassing the voice of those aspiring to the Knowledge of the Buddha [167]), essential [168]), surpassing passsion; indivisible, surpassing hatred [169]); steadfast, surpassing infatuation [170]);

11) explained by the indication of emptiness, unborn, surpass-

---

[164]) Ch.: „not oscillating (*wu tung chuan* = *viprakampya*)".

[165]) *prapañca* — the illusion about the existence of a plurality of individual entities corresponding to the ideas. Ch. adds: „ineffable (*nirabhilāpya*), because surpassing voice (*ghoṣasamatikrānta*).

[166]) *aniketa* = T. *gnas-med-pa*, literally „homeless". K.: *gnas-med-pa ni gzuṅ-ba'i gnas med-pa'i phyir-ro* // = „placeless, because having no attainable place". Cf. the Hymn of Nāgārjuna edited by T u c c i, JRAS, April 1932, p. 324, stanza 7:

na dūre nâpi câsanne nâkāśe nâpi vā kṣitau
na saṃsāre na nirvāṇe 'sthitāya namo 'stu te.

But this epithet should not be understood in the sense of the inextensionality of the Absolute. Cf. the remarks of S. S c h a y e r (*Das Mahāyānistische Absolutum*, col. 405, 406 and *Precanonical Buddhism* p. 127 f.), who proves that „the Indian philosophy from the Āraṇyakās to the Vedānta has never conceived the Soul, the Consciousness and the psychical phenomena otherwise than spatially". The Body of the Buddha is not localized, because it is omnipresent.

Ch. translates: „placeless, because homeless (*li k'u che* = *nirālaya*, a usual synonym of *aniketa*, see e. g. *Milindapañha*, p. 244)" and adds: „homeless (*wu k'u che* = *anālaya*), because unutterable (*avacya*); unsupported (*anāśrita*), because surpassing all the doctrines (*chien* = *darśana*); undefiled (*anāsrava*), because surpassing all the results (*pao* = *vipāka*)".

[167]) Ch. om., cf. the foot-note 165.

[168]) *sāraga*. The Mss. give *sarāśā* and *sarāgo*, but the T. *sñiṅ-po* and the Ch. *chien ku* warrant the connection with *sāra* and justify the emendation. The faulty form *sarāga* can easily be explained by a confusion with the *rāgasamatikrānta* which follows immediately. T. joins *sārago* with *rāgasamatikrānto* (and later *abhedyo* with *doṣasamatikrānto* and *dhruvo* with *mohasamatikrānto*). K. tries to explain this connection: *sñiṅ-po ni 'dod-chags-la-sogs-pa dri-ma'i ṅo-bo-daṅ-bral-ñid-do* // = „essential (properly speaking „clarified") [means that it is] free from impurities like passion, etc.". See the following foot-note.

[169]) K.: *dbyer-mi-phyed-pa ni źe-sdaṅ-gi mtshon-chas-so* // = „indivisible [which means that it cannot be split] with the sword of hatred".

[170]) *dhruvo doṣasamatikrānto* is missing in the Sanskrit Mss., but it must be restored on the evidence of both the translations (Ch. translates *dhruva*: „with firm and right *jñāna*"). K.: *brtan-pa ni gti-mug-gi rluṅ-gis mi-bskyod-pa-ñid-do* // = „steadfast, [that means] unshaken by the wind of infatuation".

ing birth, eternal from the standpoint of common experience [171]), undifferentiated in the aspect of Nirvāṇa [172]), described in words as suppressed [173]), quiescent in voice [174]), homogenous with regard to conventional Truth, conventional with regard to the Absolute Truth [175]), absolute according to the true teaching,

12) cool, unscorched [176]) placeless [177]), unthinkable [178]), blame-

---

171) *nityo vyāhāreṇa.* T. instead of *nitya* gives *brtags-pa* = *parīkṣita*, but in K. we find *rtag-pa* = *nitya*. K.: *rtag-pa ni tha-sñad tsam-du mi-'gyur-ba'i rtag-pa-ñid-do* // = „The eternity of something which does not exist [can be stated] only from the standpoint of common experience (or in conversation)". *tha-sñad*= *vyavahāra* can mean „conversation", see Obermiller *The Sublime Science*, p. 133; in our text *vyāhāra* is often translated simply as *brjod* „words". Ch. translates „impermanent (sic! *wu ch'ang* = *anitya*) only in words (*tan yen shuo* = *vyavahāreṇaiva*).

172) K.: *mya-ṅan-las-'das-pa-la saṅs-rgyas daṅ / ñan-thos daṅ / raṅ-saṅs-rgyas-kyi mya-ṅan-las-'das-pa'i bye-brag-med-pa-ñid-do* // = „In the *nirvāṇa* there is no distinction between the Buddhas, the Śrāvakas and the Pratyekabuddhas." Are we to understand this statement in the sense of *ekayāna* (cf. *The Doctrine of Pr. P.*, p. 29)? Ch. om.

173) K.: *sgras mya-ṅan-las-'das-pa ni sgras brjod-du-med-pa'o* // = „suppressed in words means ineffable". Ch. *ch'u li sheng ti* = *śabdabhūmivigama* (?) Cf. the subsequent foot-note.

174) K.: *brjod-bya'i rnam-par-rtogs-pa źi bas źi-ba'o* // = „quiescent owing to the quiescence of all the speech-constructions". Ch. translates exactly *śānta ghoṣeṇa* and adds *yu yin sheng i ssŭ hsiang ku* „having sounds in the thought (*ssŭ hsiang* = *cintā*) [of those who hear them]". This seems to be a Docetic explanation of *śabdabhūmivigama* (cf. the preceding note) and *śānto ghoṣeṇa*: the sounds of the preaching are unreal and exist only in the mind of the hearers (cf. the f.-note 61).

175) Ch. corresponds to: *samānyo* (*t'ung ssŭ hsiang* = *samacitta* ?) *saṃketena, vyāhāreṇa paramārtho*, and here ends the § 12. K. argues as follows: „all the definitions of the Body of Tathāgata (like existence, non-existence, etc.) are but thought-constructions, are conventional, and therefore conventionality is the common feature of all the phenomena (*samānyaḥ saṃketena*). Thus the phenomenal reality is conventional with regard to the Absolute Truth".

176) T. corresponds to *śītalo niṣparidāhena*. But K.: *bsil-ba daṅ yoṅs-su-gduṅ-ba-med-pa źes bya-ba ni ñon-moṅs-pa'i tsha-ba'i yoṅs-su-gduṅ-ba-med-pa'i phyir-ro* // = „cool and unscorched, because it is not scorched by the heat of the *kleśas*.

177) Ch. om.

178) As for the form of the Past Participle *manyito*, based on the Present stem, see F. Edgerton, Language, vol. 13, Nr. 2, 1937, p. 112. The T. translation *gźal-du-med-pa* possibly relies on the reading *amāpito* (?). Ch. om.

less[179]), infinite in terms of colours[180]), born of the application[181]) of the great supernatural faculty —thus is the Body of the Tathāgata to be called".

13) Then the Lord uttered, at this hour, this verse:

„Let him who wishes to know the Body of the Ruler of the World[182]) practise this *samādhi*, and he will cognize the Body of the Buddha.

14) Born of merits is the Body of the Buddha, pure and radiant[183]); it resembles Space[184]), and in it there is no plurality.

15) Just as is the Enlightenment of the Buddha, so are his marks[185]); and just as are the marks, so is his Body[186]).

---

179) T. and Ch. om. *anindito*. But it is found in K. *smad-du-med-pa.*

180) K.: *yon-tan brjod-pa-las mtha'-med-pa'i phyir-ro* // = „because [it appears to be] infinite, when one enumerates its features *(guṇa)*". Cf. §§ 40—45. Ch. om. but adds instead: „absolute according to the true teaching (cf. the end of the § 12), unscorched as being in Nirvāṇa (*niṣparidāho nirvāṇena*), indestructible (*wu yu huai* = *avināśa?)*, invincible (*wu neng sheng* = *ajeya*) unattached (*wu ts'ü chu* = *anadhyavasita*), having attained Nirvāṇa in the sense of the *prapañca* (*mieh hsi lun i ku*), free from illusional differentiation (*niṣprapañca*) as having no objects of cognition (*li p'an yüan* = *nirālambana*), infinite when its merits (*fu* = *puṇya*, possibly also a confusion with *guṇa*, cf. the K. to *aparyanto varṇanirdeśena* quoted above) are to be enumerated, having no atoms, because it is tought as being subtle (? *wu yu wei ch'en shuo wei hsi ku*)".

181) *parikarma* = T. *yoṅs-su-sbyoṅ-ba* = Ch. *pen yeh* „preparations, appliances connected with the ten stages of the Bodhisattva" cf. *The Doctrine of Pr. P.*, p. 53, 54, 84. Ch. adds: „endowed with selfmastery, as having the majesty (*prabhāva*) (*te tzŭ yu tzŭ tsai li ku*), indestructible, because of its hardness (*wu p'o huai i chien shih ku*), infinite, because its names are inexhaustible (*wu tsin* = *akṣaya*), [this Body] preaches elaborately because of its application (*parikarma*) to the great Compassion".

182) Note the Ch. term for *lokanātha* (*shih men ts'in*).

183) K.: *raṅ-bzin-gyis 'od-gsal-ba-ñid-do / rmoṅs-pa'i mun-pa-med-pa'i phyir-ro* // = „it is radiant in its essence, as being not obscured by delusion".

184) K.: ... *bar-snaṅ-mtshuṅs-pa ni spros-pa-med-pas-so* = „it resembles Space, because it is not differentiated in illusory separate elements (*niṣprapañca*)".

185) The 32 marks of the Mahāpuruṣa. K.: *gal-te mtshan-sum-cu-rtsa-gñis-daṅ-ldan-pa'i de-bzin-gśegs-pa'i mṅon-par-byaṅ-chub-sku n.ña'-na ci-ltar bar-snaṅ-mtshuṅs-pa'i sku yin źe-na... ci-ltar sku gzod-ma-nas źi-ba yin-pa de-ltar mtshan-rnams kyaṅ yin-la saṅs-rgyas-kyi źiṅ-rnams kyaṅ de-daṅ-'dra'o* // = „if the *abhisambodhikāya* of the Tathāgata is endowed with 32 marks, how can it resemble Space?... Just as the Body is quiescent from the outset, so quiescent are its marks and the spheres of the Buddha".

186) Cf. *The Doctrine of. Pr. P.*, p. 112: „... Enlightenment (*bodhi* = *byaṅ-*

16) The mark of the Body is Enlightenment and is that of the spheres of the Buddha. Powers [187]), stages of emancipation [188]), concentrations [189])—they all have only this one mark[190]).

17) Such is the nature of the Buddhas, Rulers of the World. Nobody can perceive them with the bodily eye.

18) Many may say: „I have seen the Leader of the World; with his golden-coloured body [191]) he illuminates the entire world".

19) But it is only thanks to the sustaining power [192]) of the Buddhas, to their magical faculty and to the miraculous transformations, that the Body adorned with marks can be seen.

20) It is tought that the Body of the Buddha has height and curcumference, but its dimensions are not grasped and therefore it is inconceivable [193]).

21) If one could grasp those dimensions, [thinking]: „The Body of the Buddha has such and such a size", the Teacher would not be different from gods and men [194]).

---

chub) viewed sub specie aeternitatis is the Cosmical Body (*dharmakāya*). The difference between this subject and the Buddhahood, is that here Enlightenment is viewed as something to be attained (by the person proceeding) on the Path himself, whereas before it has been taken from the standpoint of the element already attained by another personality..." Ch.: „and just as its marks are inapprehensible, so is the Body of the Tathāgata".

187) *bala* = T. *stobs* = Ch. *li*.

188) *vimokṣa* = *rnam-(par)-thar-(ba)* = Ch. *chiai t'o*.

189) *dhyāna* = T. *bsam-gtan* = Ch. *shan*. In Ch. *shan* precedes *chiai t'o*.

190) According to K. this one mark is the absence of marks [from the standpoint of the absolute Truth] (*mtshan-ñid-med-par mtshan-ñid-gcig-pa żes bya'o*). Cf. § 45 and the foot-note 44.

191) Ch. „... with his incomparable, marvellous, golden-coloured body..."

192) *adhiṣṭhāna* = T. *byin-brlabs* = Ch. *chia* „the power of Buddha by means of which he sustains beings anf helps them to attain salvat on. Here *ādhiṣṭhānikī ṛddhi* „the power of appearing anywhere and in any form" (cf. *Aspects*, p. 111) is meant.

193) Ch. „The marks of breadth and length can be seen in the world, but his marks (of the Buddha) are invisible. If one could know the marks of the Body, there should be no difference between the Buddha and the world".

194) Ch. „If one could grasp the dimensions of the Body od Buddha, thinking: these are all the Tathāgatas, then there should be no difference between the Body of Buddha and what is not the Body [of Buddha]; similarly [there should be no difference between the Buddha] and men and gods (*hsiu-lo* = *sura*)".

22) The result of the perfectly concentrated mind has the same mark [195]); and the *nāma-rūpa* has that mark too; it becomes pure and radiant.

23) No one has ever [196]) practised this holy *samādhi* so well as it is practised by the Ruler of the World for millions of aeons [197]).

24) This *samādhi* is born of many bright *dharmas;* owing to the enormity of this *samādhi,* my body cannot be perceived.

25) Just as is the mind of someone, so is his *nāma-rūpa.* If the mind is unsubstantial [198]), the *nāma-rūpa* has also the same mark [199]).

26) If in the *nāma-rūpa* of someone there works a coarse [200]) *saṃjñā,* etc., then, since this *saṃjñā* is not homogenous [with the pure mind], the mind becomes coarse too.

27) But, if in the *nāma-rūpa* of someone there works

---

195) K.: *spros-pa thams-cad daṅ / ñe-bar-bral-ba'i sems ni mñam-par-gżug-pa'o // de'i rnam-par-smin-pa'i sems kyaṅ de-daṅ-'dra-ba-ste...* = „The mind free from any illusional differentiation is perfectly concentrated. The consciousness resulting from it is equally concentrated". In Ch. the reading *kuo* of the „Three ed.", „the old Sung ed." and „the Shôgo-zô Mss." is to be introduced in the place of i_4 adopted by the Taishô editors. *Samāhita* is rendered by *k'ung chi* which means rather *śūnya* (cf. Rosenberg, *Introd. to the Study of Buddhism, Vocabulary,* p. 358).

196) Narendrayaśas, as it seems, has read *jñātu* instead of *jātu* and has translated: „No one is known who practised this holy *samādhi,* but the Ruler of the World, etc...".

197) According to the Docetic conception of the Buddhahood, the Tathāgata is constantly in *samādhi,* cf. *Laṅkāvatāra,* p. 240: *sadā samāhitāś ca Tathāgatāḥ.*

198) Ch., contrary to the translation of XIX, 16 (cf. the foot-note 114), reads *visabhāga* (*lui ming pu t'ung*) instead of *nisvabhāva.* This faulty reading could easily arise from the confusion with *visabhāga* which occurs in the subsequent stanza of the original text where in Ch. it is not translated.

199) Note the identification of *nāma-rūpa* with *citta,* cf. the § 22. K.: *sems-kyi ṅo-bo-ñid-med-pas miṅ-daṅ-gzugs kyaṅ ṅo-bo-ñid-med-pa /* = „the mind being unsubstantial, the *nāma-rūpa* is unsubstantial too".

200) *udāra* = Pali *oḷārika,* T. *rags-pa,* Ch. *ts'u-ta* „coarse, rough". Ch. translates: „If some one has a coarse *saṃjñā,* then he has a corresponding *nāma-rūpa;* if the *nāma-rūpa* is coarse, then a corresponding *saṃjñā* arises".

a subtle[201]) *saṃjñā*, then his mind becomes radiant and unfastened to the *nāma-rūpa*[202]).

28) I recollect, in my former lives, during the seven „immeasurable periods" [203]) the three evil *saṃjñā*[204]) never arose in me.

29) Undefiled[205]) is my mind, for I save the beings dur-

---

201) *mṛduka* = T. *phra-mo* = Ch. *wei hsí.*

202) A purified consciousness is no more fastened to the individual *nāma-rūpa* (cf. p. 26). Ch.: „When some one has a subtle *saṃjñā*, then he has a similar *nāma-rūpa;* if his *nāma-rūpa* is unattached (*pu-chu* = *agṛddha*), the Body of his mind is radiant".

The §§ 25—27 seem to have some doctrinal importance. According to them *saṃjñā* can be of different kinds, more or less subtle and the degree of subtleness depends on the mind. This thesis is entirely incompatible with the axioms of the dharma-theory: the immutability and the absolute individuality *(pṛthaktva)* of all the elements. Such conceptions can be met with as early as in the Sautrāntika school. Vasubandhu, when asked why the *skandhas* are always enumerated in a definite order, replies (AK. I, II. p. 42): *kramaḥ punaḥ/ yathaudārika saṃkleśabhajanādyārthadhātutaḥ* = „this order corresponds to the [degrees of] coarseness...". But if the *skandhas* can be classified with regard to their coarseness, then this gradation presupposes the existence of a conception (not expressly stated by Vasubandhu) that all those elements have a certain homogeneity and affinity. It is expressed clearer in another place of he AK (I,II,p.173) where Vasubandhu expounds the views of the Sautrāntikas on the dharmas *caitta: vitarka vicara audaryasukṣmate* which means that those different dharmas *vitarka* and *vicara* are one and the same consciousness differing only in the degrees of its subtleness. Here we have a rejection, still not quite conscious, of the *pṛthakva*. J. Masuda (*Origin and Doctrines of early Indian Buddhist Schools*, p. 68, f.-note 1, concerning the so called *ekarasaskandha*) quotes the views of the Sautrāntikas, according to which all the *skandhas*, even *rūpa*, arise from consciousness.

In the above stanzas the connection between *nāma-rūpa* and *citta* is not clearly defined, but in any case it consists in a close interdependence. A special emphasis is laid on *saṃñjā*, the modifications of which depend on the fundamental, hence non-individual (*agṛddhaṃ nāma-rūpasmi*) *cittaṃ prabhāsvaram* (see p. 26). Even the 3 *kleśas* are not, as in the dharma-theory, three separate elements accompanying consciousness, but are modifications of this consciousness, its defilement through which it is rendered coarse (*udāra*). According to the § 28, the 3 *kleśas* are merely variations of the *saṃjñā* (cf. the f.-note 204). Hence, both *saṃñjā* and *nāma-rūpa* are so closely allied with the *citta*, that this conception can be called *cittamātratā*.

203) Ch. during 70 „immeasurable periods".

204) According to K., these are the 3 *kleśas*: *rāga*, *dveṣa* and *moha*.

205) *anāsrava* „free from the *kleśas* (cf. the preceding stanza and the f.-note 204) from passion and will to live (*Ausgewählte Kapitel*, p. 58 note B).

ing the inconceivable millions of aeons. And therefore my Body cannot be perceived.

30) He whose mind is freed from all the *bhāvas*, has no more contact with those *bhāvas*.

31) Fully delivered from all *bhāvas* is my consciousness,—realized is the essence of the mind, and greater becomes my knowledge.

32) Thousands of millions of the spheres are magically created by me, and they serve the beings. Even there my Body cannot be grasped.

33) Markless, signless, as is the sky—thus is defined my Body which is ineffable and hard to understand.

34) The Great Hero is identical with the Absolute Body. Born [206]) of *dharma* is his body; the Victorious One cannot be conceived in the aspect of the Material Body [207]).

35) To him who, having heard this teaching, is rejoiced[208]), Māra the evil one [209]) will not have any opportunity to do harm [210]).

36) And he who, having heard this profound Truth, is not frightened, will never reject [211]), for life's sake, the Enlightenment of the Buddha.

37) From millions of the sūtras will he learn the teaching conforming to Truth, and wherever he will go, he will be the Light of men.

38) Then, o Kumāra, it is not easy to comprehend the Body

---

[206]) *nirjito*. T. *skyes-pa* and Ch. *sheng* corroborate the meaning „born". This strange form is probably a blend of *nirjāta* and *nirmita* which occurs in the § 32.

[207]) Cf. *Vajracchedikā*, p. 43:

dharmato buddhā draṣṭavyā dharmakāyā hi nāyakāḥ
dharmatā câpy avijñeyā na sā śakyā vijānitum.

(cf. *Precanonical Buddhism*, p. 126).

[208]) Literally: „who will have the delight of hearing this teaching".

[209]) As for the Ch. transcription *po sun* = *pāpīyan*, cf. J. Przyluski, *Le Concile de Rājagṛha*, Buddhica II, Paris, 1926—28, p. 14, f.-note 1, and P. Pelliot T'oung Pao, XXX, 1933, pp. 85-99.

[210]) *avatāram labhiṣyati* = Ch. *te ch'i pien*. In T. all the xylographs give *glan-ka* probably a mistake which I am correcting into the usual *glags*.

[211]) Ch: „will not slander (*pu fei pang*) the Enlightenment of the Buddha".

of the Tathāgata even through his marks [212]), and determine whether it is blue, or blue-coloured, or apparently blue, or bluelike; whether it is yellow, yellow-coloured, etc... red,... white,... scarlet [213]),... crystal-like,... flame-like,... ghee-like [214])),... golden,... vaidurya-like,... lightening-like,... Brahma-like,... god-like [215]). Thus [216]), o Kumāra, the Body of the Tathāgata is pure, inconceivable even by its marks, defined as inconceivable, inconceivable in all its marks, and the examples [for this Body] are inconceivable.

39) As for the Material Body in its full perfection, it would not be easy to find in the world including even gods a definition for this Body, unless one describes it as inconceivable and undefinable in all its aspects" [217]).

40) Then the Lord uttered, at this hour, this verse:

„As many as there are specks of dust designed under the

---

[212]) According to K., this statement concerns the *sambhogakāya: de-ni loṅs-spyod-rdzogs-pa'i sku yaṅ zab-ciṅ rgya-che-ba yin-no źes bstan-pa'i phyir / gźon-nu de-la de-bźin-gśegs-pa'i sku ni źes bya-ba-la-sogs-pa gsuṅs-te/* = „It is said: 'Then, o Kumāra, the Body of the Tathagata etc.' in order to point out that the *saṃbhogakāya* is profound and immense". But in the text *rūpakāya*, as proved by the § 39, is meant. In the *Samādhirājasūtra* the *saṃbhogakāya* is not mentioned at all, but, as I have already emphasized (p. 24), the *rūpakāya* is endowed with features which later characterize the *saṃbhogakāya.*

[213]) *mañjiṣṭha.* T. *le-brgan* „poppy-coloured", Ch. *hung tzŭ* „purple". Here are enumerated the five colours regarded as fundamental in India and China. Cf. the Hymn of Nagārjuna, already referred to (JRAS, 1932, p. 322, stanza 5):

na rakto haritamāñjiṣṭho varṇas te nopalabhyate
na pītakṛṣṇaśuklo vā 'varṇāya namo 'stu te.

[214]) *sarpimaṇḍo* „creem of ghee", T. *mar* „butter, oil". In Ch. the reading su_2 (=*ghṛta*) of the Ming edition is to be substituted to su_1 (= *soma*) reading of all the other Mss. and of the Taishô ed.

[215]) Ch interchanges *deva* (*t'ien*) and *brahma* (*fan*).

[216]) Ch., beginning from here, means: „Such is the Body of the Tathāgata: immeasurable in all its marks, inconceivable, ineffable".

[217]) Ch.: „As for the full perfection of the Material Body, all the gods and men cannot fathom it. [They cannot know] in details whether it is long or short, wide or narrow. It is illimited, inconceivable, incalculable". K.: *gzugs-kyi sku'i ṅes-pa yaṅ yoṅs-su-gzuṅ-ba daṅ / tshad bzuṅ-bar ni lha daṅ bcas-pa'i 'jig-rten-gyis kyaṅ sla-ba ma-yin-na yaṅ chos-kyi sku lta-smos kyaṅ ci-dgos /* = „To conceive the true nature (*ṅes-pa*) even of the Material Body, it would not be easy to find a definition (*tshad*) of it in the world including gods, — to say nothing of the Absolute Body!"

name[218]) of powder, as many as there are water-drops in springs, ponds, lakes, and oceans,

41) so many are the atoms,—and their number cannot be grasped. Even if one could count with the point of a hair[219]) the water-drops,

42) one could not find a comparison equal[220]) to the Ruler of the World. But the water-drops are incalculable, so are the atoms too,

43) and in one single being I see still more [mental dispositions like] the rise of the thought endowed with faith. It is impossible to comprehend [all those elements] at once[221]).

---

[218]) *saṃjñā* = T. *miṅ.*

[219]) *vālakoṭi* = T. *skra-rtse-(mo)* = *vālāgra* „a measure = 8 *rajas* = 64 *paramāṇu*".

[220]) The Mss. give *tu yāval, tu yā.* I propose the emendation *tulyā* which may correspond to the T. *ruṅ.* Ch. translates: „For the Leader Tathāgata such a comparison is quoted".

[221]) K. interpretes the stanzas 40—44 as follows: *'jig-rten khams-kyi khams thams-cad-kyi rdul-phra-rab-ni bgraṅ-bar nus kyaṅ srid / skra'i rtse-mo brgyar bśags-pas rgya-mtsho chen-po'i chu-thig-pa bgraṅ-bar nus kyaṅ srid-kyi de-bźin-gśegs-pa'i yaṅ-dag-pa'i yon-tan bsṅags-pa brjod-par mi-nus-so // de'i phyir 'jig-rten-gyi khams ma-lus-pa'i 'byuṅ-ba-chen-po lṅa'i rdul-phra-rab ji-sñed yod-pa de-bas kyaṅ sems-can gcig-gi sems-kyi spyod-pa maṅ-bar mthoṅ-ṅo // de-bźin-du sems-can thams-cad-kyi sems-kyi spyod-pa'i khyad-par de-dag kyaṅ ṅa'i yaṅ-dag-pa'i yon-tan-gyi bsṅags-pa'i dper bzod-pa ma-yin-no //* = „Even if one could count the atoms of all the worlds of the Universe, even if one could count with the point of a hair split in hundred parts the water-drops of the ocean,—yet, it would be impossible to praise in words the real features (*guṇa*) of the Tathāgata. Therefore, no matter how numerous may be the atoms of the 5 great elements (*mahābhūta*) of the entire Universe, in one single being a greater number of mental dispositions (*citta-caryā*) is perceived. And even the mental dispositions of all the different beings cannot serve as a comparison for the praising of my (of the Tathāgata) real features".

We have here the following climax: a) the water-drops and the atoms are innumerable, b) there are still more mental dispositions (cf. Obermiller, *The Sublime Science*, p. 154) in one single being, c) the features of the Tathāgata are more numerous than the mental dispositions of all the beings. This simple idea is expressed in a rather intricate way, and it is not quite sure whether the commentator did not read into those stanzas more than they contain. These verses offered difficulties to the translators, and T. and Ch. differ considerably. The end of the stanza 43 is translated in T. as follows: „faith is the *citta-utpāda* (?). These [elements?] are numerous and not easy to comprehend". It is possible that the T. translator has read (with BC): °*cittautpado 'nekakāle prajānitum*, and *du-ma-dag* would correspond to this

44) But no comparison is possible between those [elements] and the real colours [222]) of my Body [223]) which I have revealed and in which all the beings believe [224]).

45) One cannot comprehend [this Body] through its marks, [saying] [225]): 'Such is the lustre of the colours of the Buddha'. And this is just my distinction [226]).

46) The Buddhas are deprived of marks, and their true Nature is the Absolute Body. They are profound and immeasurable and therefore they are inconceivable.

47) The Body of the inconceivable Buddha is also inconceivable. For these inconceivable bodies, as their true nature, have the Absolute Body.

48) Even thought cannot conceive the Body of the Buddhas; therefore there exists no mode of knowing this body.

49) Those immeasurable *dharmas* were cultivated for millions of aeons, and therefore my Body is inconceivable, radiant and in the state of Nirvāṇa.

50) Incomprehensible to all beings, it cannot be grasped through any mode of cognition; thus is the Body of the Buddha, unknowable and inconceivable.

---

*aneka*⁰. The Ch. translator has read *ekakāle* (*i shih*) and understood the stanza 43 as follows: „In one single being (I adopt, against Taishô, the reading *i chung sheng* of the „Three editions" and the „Old Sung ed.") I see a greater number of atoms. Out of this thought arises the faith and this can be comprehended in one moment". But the reading *naikakāle* seems the most likely. It means that those elements are not inconceivable in their very nature, but are too numerous to be comprehended at once. Like the features of the *rūpakāya* they are inexhaustible, cf. p. 24 and the foot-note 180. Cf. also *Samādhirājasūtra*, the Xth chpt. (*Purapraveśa*): *buddhaprātihārya na sukaru vaktu ca kalpakoṭiyebhiḥ*.

222) Cf. the § 38. T. *yon-tan* = *guṇa*.

223) *ātmabhāva* = *kāya*, cf. *Bodhicaryāvatāra*, Bibl. Ind. p. 80, the commentary of Prajñākāramati, the f.-note 2 and the p. 95, f.-note 1.

224) This stanza is not less difficult in its syntax. The literal meaning may be: „As for the real colours of my Body which I have revealed (and all the beings believe in them), there cannot be any comparison between those (*tān*) [elements] and these (*eteṣām*) [colours]". *adhimukta* can be constructed with the accusative, cf. *Dhammapada* 226: *nibbānaṃ adhimuttānaṃ*. Ch. may mean: „As for the external colours of my Body which were revealed, all the beings wishing to believe in them cannot find a fit comparison for them".

225) I adopt the interpretation of T. which has the particle *źes*.

226) „...that this Body cannot be defined through its marks". Cf. XXII, 16 and the f.-note 190.

51) For this [Body] the mode of cognition is constructed of the unknowable *dharmas*[227]; as these *dharmas* are not constructed, the idea of the Buddha cannot be constructed too.

52) As it was stated that cognition is a mental construction, all that is unconstructed, is unknowable. Therefore the Buddha who cannot be constructed and is beyond all mental constructions, is inconceivable.

53) Just as Space is immeasurable and cannot be measured by any one, so is the Buddha, exactly like Space.

54) And those who thus conceive the Body, are the sons of the Victorious Ones; they will become Buddhas too, inconceivable Rulers of the World[228].

---

[227]) Ch. agrees with the original text, but the reading *sui* of the Taishô ed has to be changed into *fo* attested in the „Three editions", the „Old Sung ed." and the „Shôgo-zô Mss." T. differs: „[Even] by means of the unknowable dharmas the mode of cognition of this [Body] cannot be constructed (*brtag-tu-med* = *akalpita*)".

[228]) In Ch. the reading *ts'in* of the „Three ed.", the „Old Sung ed." and the „Shôgo-zô Mss." must be substituted to *tu*, which was adopted by the Taishô editors.

TRZY ROZDZIAŁY Z SAMĀDHIRĀJASŪTRY.

STRESZCZENIE POLSKIE.

Z pomiędzy „9 dharm" nepalskich *Samādhirājasūtra* jest jedynym większym tekstem dotąd niewydanym w całości i bardzo mało znanym; wydaje się to tym dziwniejsze, że musiał to być tekst o wielkim znaczeniu, jak o tym świadczą liczne cytaty w późniejszej literaturze buddyjskiej zwłaszcza w dziełach Candrakīrtiego i Śāntidevy.

Ponieważ prof. Stanisław Schayer zamierza opracować wraz ze mną krytyczne wydanie całego tekstu, praca niniejsza ma charakter raczej przygotowawczy i zawiera krytyczne wydanie wraz z przekładem i komentarzem trzech rozdziałów (VIII, XIX i XXII), *Samādhirājasūtry* mających dość duże znaczenie dla poznania doktrynalnego stanowiska tekstu. Niewielkie stosunkowo rozmiary badanego tekstu pozwoliły na bardziej szczegółowe potraktowanie strony językowej i metrycznej, na dosyć drobiazgowe porównanie oryginału z tybetańskim i chińskim przekładem oraz na szersze uwzględnienie komentarza Mañjuśrīkīrtiego do *Samādhirājasūtry* p. t. *Kīrtimala* (zachowanego jedynie w tybetańskim przekładzie).

W pracy mojej oparłem się na czterech rękopisach nepalskich (z Bibliothèque Nationale w Paryżu: fonds sanskr. 143, 144/145, 146 i z University Library w Cambridge, sansk. ms. add. 916) oraz na dwóch wersjach: pekińskiej i narthangskiej przekładu tybetańskiego (dokonanego przez Śīlendrabodhiego i Dharmatāśīlę w IX wieku).

Z trzech znanych i wydanych w Taishô przekładów chińskich uwzględniam wyłącznie przekład Narendrayaśasa z 557 roku (Taishô 639), jako jedyny, w którym znajdują się badane rozdziały. W przeciwieństwie do wersyj tybetańskich ściśle zgadzających się z oryginałem, przekład chiński zawiera liczne odchylenia od tekstu sanskryckiego i jest naogół krótszy. Porównanie przekładów i ich dat pozwala ustalić w przybliżeniu epokę powstania *Samādhirājasūtry*. Sam tekst o tym tytule musiał być skompilowany nie później od

IV-go wieku po Chr., a pewne archaizmy doktrynalne pozwalają na umieszczenie jego jeszcze wcześniej, w epoce kształtowania się *Prājñāparamitāsūtr*, około III wieku po Chr. W VII-mym wieku *Samādhirājasūtra* musiała mieć mniej więcej dzisiejszą postać, jak o tym świadczą cytaty pochodzące z tej epoki. Z całą pewnością jednak stwierdzić to można dopiero dla IX wieku, kiedy powstał przekład tybetański, ściśle odpowiadający rękopisom indyjskim w ich dzisiejszym stanie.

Pod względem językowym *Samādhirājasūtra*, zwłaszcza jej partie metryczne, dostarcza bardzo obfitego materiału dla badań t. zw. „buddyjskiego sanskrytu". Z r. dszych form zacytować można: acc. plur. masc. na *ă* : *varṣa acintiya* XIX, 24, gen. sing. *samādhiya* XIX, 27, acc. sing. od *mātar*: *mātāṃ* VIII, 7, gen. plur. *sarvāṇa* VIII, 22, 24, aorysty typu *kurviṣu* XXII, 4, absolutyw *sthihitvā* VIII, 22, słowa jak *upīḍa* XIX, 17, 18, *avaśya* XXII, 6 i t. d. Jeszcze cenniejsze są gāthy *Samādhirājasūtry* pod względem prozodycznym i metrycznym. Znajdujemy tam bardzo interesującą i ważną dla dalszego rozwoju metryki mahajanistycznej a nieznaną w epoce wcześniejszej odmianę *Upendravajry* = ⏓ — ⏑ ⏑ ⏑ — ⏑ ⏑ — ⏑ — — (VIII, 7b, c). Niemniej ważne są przykłady bardzo archaicznej *Protododhaki* — ⏑ — ⏑ | ⏑ ⏑ — | ⏑ ⏑ | ⏓ (XIX, 19b d.).

Pod względem doktrynalnym ma *Samādhirājasūtra* pierwszorzędne znaczenie dla poznania zbyt mało dotąd zbadanych koncepcyj wczesnej Mahajany, kiedy rozdział pomiędzy idealistycznymi tezami Vijñānavādinów a agnostycyzmem dyskursywnym Mādhyamików jeszcze się nie wytworzył z całą przejrzystością. Tematem tekstu jest raczej werbalne „rozwijanie" niż filozoficzna analiza zasadniczej tezy o „identyczności wszystkich dharm w ich istocie", tezy będącej podstawą głównej medytacji, t. zw. „Króla medytacyj (*samādhirāja*) Wobec tego, że to „rozwijanie" (któremu odpowiada termin *vipañcita*) ma charakter czysto słownego wyliczania najrozmaitszych aspektów owej identyczności, wartość doktrynalną ma nie tyle treść zasadnicza tekstu, ile ubocznie poruszane inne tezy. Takim ubocznym tezom, a mianowicie doktrynie o ciałach Buddy, o nieistnieniu wszystkich dharm, o czystej i jaśniejącej świadomości i t. d. są poświęcone rozdziały stanowiące temat niniejszej pracy.

Samādhirājasūtra uchodzi za podstawowy tekst szkoły Mādhyamików. Znajdujemy tam istotnie wszystkie typowe tezy *śūnyavādy* i teorię ciał Buddy, zbliżoną do koncepcji *Prajñāpāramitāsūtr*. Nasz tekst zna jedynie dwa ciała: *dharmakāya* i *rūpakāya*. Charakterystyczna dla późnej *Vijñānavādy* koncepcja *sambhogakāyi* jeszcze nie istnieje i atrybuty tego trzeciego ciała są w *Samādhirājasūtrze* podzielone pomiędzy dwa pozostałe ciała.

Z innej jednak strony nie można zaprzeczyć, że stanowisko *Samādhirājasūtry* nie wyczerpuje się w tezach *śūnyavādy* i zawiera wyraźnie sformułowane koncepcje idealistyczne. Rozdz. XIX interpretuje tezę o identyczności wszystkich dharm w sensie idealistycznym: „wszystkie dharmy są identyczne, ponieważ opierają się na tym samym elemencie, na jednym włosku". Komentator identyfikuje ten włosek ze świadomością, a dowodem na to, że nie deformuje zasadniczej tendencji tekstu, mogą być strofki 26—37 rodz. XXII, gdzie postulowana jest identyczność *nāma-rūpa* = *citta*, oparta na tym założeniu, że zarówno *nāma-rūpa*, jak też np. *saṃjñā* są derywatami czystej świadomości.

Koncepcje podobne, odnajdujące się już w bardzo starych warstwach buddyzmu (np. *Ṣaddhātusūtra*, por. St. Schayer *Precanonical Buddhism*, str. 125), implikują traktowanie świadomości jako jedynego, wiecznego, podstawowego elementu, z którego się wszystko pozostałe wyłania. t. zw. *ādiśuddha, prabhāsvara ekacitta*.

W ten sposób okazuje się, że *Samādhirājasūtra* nie reprezentuje ani radykalnej *śūnyavādy*, ani rozwiniętej *vijñānavādy* i nie może być umieszczona w żadnej z trzech epok rozwojowych buddyzmu, „trzech poruszeń koła", ustalonych przez historiografów tybetańskich i przyjmowanych przez szkołę leningradzką. Wobec tego, że mamy podobne trudności przy klasyfikacji takich tekstów jak *Avataṃsaka*, *Śrīmālādevīsūtra*, *Vimalakīrtinirdeśa* i t. d., należy przyznać, że ten potrójny schemat nie odpowiada prawdzie, ujmując w zbyt sztywne ramy płynny rozwój idei filozoficznych. Dane zawarte w powyższych tekstach, łącznie z *Samādhirājasūtrą*, każą nam przypuścić, że we wczesnym okresie Mahajany panowała ogólno-mahajanistyczna metafizyka, łącząca negatywną *śūnyavādę* z pozytywno-idealistyczną koncepcją *dharmakāya* = *dharmadhātu* = *citta prabhāsvara*. O dalszych szczegółach tej doktryny pouczyć może ściślejsze zbadanie wymienionych tekstów, które po większej części jeszcze nawet nie są wydane.

INDEX

INDEX

SANSKRIT — TIBETAN — CHINESE.

The words are specified with the letters T. or Ch. only when one of the equivalents is missing. When the Sanskrit word is missing in the original text, its presupposed reconstruction is included in square brackets [ ].

I.

Proper Names.

II.

Technical Terms and Expressions.

akalpita=*ma-brtags-pa* XXII.51, *rtog-pa-med* XXII.52=*wu yu fen pieh* XXII.51.52.
akalpya = *mi-rtog* = *wu fen pieh* XXII.52.
akuśala = *mi-dge-ba* = *pu shan* XXII.2.
[*akṣaya*] = Ch. *wu tsin* XXII.12.
agṛddha = *ma-chags-pa* = *pu chu* XXII.27.
agrāhya = *gzuṅ-du-med* = *wu neng ts'ü* XXII.50.
acala = *mi-gyo-ba* = *wu tung yao* XXII.9.
acintya = *bsam-(gyis)-mi-khyab-(pa)* VIII.8, XIX.1—5, 14, 15, 35, 37, XXII.10, 20, 38, 39, 46, 50, *bsam-du-med* XXII.47, 49, 52, *bsam-yas* VIII.21, XXII.29 = *pu k'o ssŭ i* VIII.8, XIX.1—3, 14, XXII.38, 39, *pu k'o ssŭ* XXII.10, 50, *pu ssŭ i* XIX.18, 19, 37, XXII.29, 46, 47, 52 *pu ssŭ* XXII.47, *wu neng ssŭ* XXII.47, *nan ssŭ* XXII.49.
ajāta = *ma-skyes-pa* = *wu yu sheng* XXII.11.
[*ajeya*] = Ch. *wu neng sheng* XXII.12.
atyantākāśasvabhāva = T. *śin-tu-nam-mkha'i ṅo-bo-ñid* XXII.9.
adṛśya = *mi-snaṅ-ba* = *pu k'o chien* XXII.9.
adhimukta (*adhimuktika*) = *mos-pa* XIX.2—4 = *shen hsin* XIX.2, 3.
adhimukti = *mos-pa* = *hsin*₁ XXII.44.
adhiṣṭhāna = *byin-brlabs* = *chia* XXII.19.
adhyavasāna = *chags-pa* = XXII.2, 6, *rab-tu-chags* XXII.4, *lhag-par-chags-pa* XXII.5 = *chu* XXII.2.
anakṣara = T. *yi-ge-med-pa* VIII.2, 6.
anadhyavasita = *ma-chags-par-'gyur* VIII.4, *ma-chags-pa* XXII.1, 3 = *pu chu* XXII.1, *wu ts'ü chu* XXII.12.
ananta = *mtha'-yas* XIX.30 = *wu yu p'ien* XIX.30, *wu p'ien* XIX.37.
[*anāśrita*] = Ch. *wu so i* XXII,10.
anāsrava = *zag-med-pa* XXII.29 = *wu chu lou* XXII.10, *wu lou* XXII.29.
aniketa = *gnas-med-pa* XXII.10, 12 = *wu chü chu* XXII.10.
[*anitya*] = Ch. *wu ch'ang* XXII.11.
anindita XXII.12.
animitta = *mtshan-ma-med-pa* VIII.2, 5, XXII.9 = *wu yu hsiang* XXII.9.
animittasvabhāva = *mtshan-ma-med-pa'i ṅo-bo-ñid* = *wu yu hsiang hsing* XXII.9.
aniruddha = T. *ma-'gags-pa* VIII.2, *'gags-pa-med* VIII.5.
anuttara = *bla-na-med-pa* VIII.1, 4, 19, 27, XXII.1, 3, 7, 37 = *wu shang* VIII.8, 17, *a nou to lo* XIX.37.
anutpanna = T. *ma-skyes-pa* VIII.2, *skyes-pa-med* VIII.5.
anubhava = *mthu* XIX.15, 19 = *li neng* XXII.19.
aparimāṇa = T. *tshad-med-pa* VIII.8, 18.
aparyanta = *mu-med-pa* = *wu yu p'ien chi* XXII.12.
apratiṣṭhita = T. *mi-gnas-pa* XXII.8.
apramāṇa = *tshad-med-pa* XXII.9, 50—53 = *nan liang* XXII.50, *wu liang* XXII.51, *wu hsien* XXII.53.
aprameya = *gźal-du-med-pa* VIII.8, *dpag-(tu)-med-(pa)* VIII.18, XIX.1, 5, 6, 8, 9, 37

XXII.39, 42, 46, 49 = wu liang VIII.8, XIX.37, wu yu hsien ch'i XXII.39, wu hsien XXII.42, wu hsien liang XXII.46,49.

abhāva = T. raṅ-bźin-med VIII.7, dṅos-po-med-(pa) VIII.1—3, 5, 6, 9—11, 22—25.

abhisaṃskāra = T. mṅon-par-'du-byed-pa XXII.2 mṅon-par-'du-bya XIX,2.

abhedya = dbyer-mi-phyed-pa = wu fen ch'i XXII.9, pu huai XXII.10.

arhant = dgra-bcom-pa VIII.8, 12—14, 17, XIX.12 = ying(kung) VIII.8—10, 17, XIX.12.

alakṣaṇa = mtshan-ñid med-pa VIII.2, 5, XXII.33 = Ch. wu hsiang XIX.16, XXII.33.

[avācya] = Ch. li yen yin XXII.10.

[avināśa] = Ch. wu yu huai, wu p'o huai XXII 12.

asaṃkhyeya = graṅs-med-pa VIII.8, 18, XIX.6, XXII.28 = wu shu VIII 8, pu k'o shu XXII 39, a seng chih VIII.8, XXII.28.

asārika = T. sñiṅ-po-med-pa XXII.5.

asvabhāva = T. ṅo-bo-ñid-med-pa VIII.2.

ākāra = rnam-pa = chung XXII.39.

ātmabhāva = sku = tzŭ shen XXII.44.

ādiśānta = T. gzod-ma-nas-źi-ba VIII.2.

ānuśaṃsa = T. phan-yon XIX.1, 5, 8, 9.

utpāda (buddhānām) = (saṅs-rgyas-rnams)-skye-źiṅ = (fo) ch'u shih XIX.22.

upīḍa = gnod-pa- 'gyur-ba = (pien) chai XIX.17, 18.

ṛddhi = rdzu-'phrul = shen li XIX.14, 15.

ekalakṣaṇa = mtshan-ñid-gcig = i $hsiang_1$ XXII.16.

ekārtha = don-gcig-tu = i i XXII 9.

karman = las VIII.30, XXII.2.

kalpa = bskal-pa VIII.8, 16, 17, 21, 29, XXII.23, 29, 49 = chieh VIII.8, 16, 17, XXII.23, 29, 49.

kalpa (= kalpana) = rtog-pa = fen pieh XXII 52.

kāya = lus XXII.1—6, 24, 29, 32, 49, sku XXII 13—16, 18—21, 33, 34, 38, 39, 47, 48, 50, = shen XXII.1, 2, 13—16, 18—21, 24, 29, 33, 34, 38, 39, 47—50, 53, 54.

kāṣāya = ṅur-smrig = chia sha VIII.15.

kuśala = mkhas-pa VIII.1—3, XIX.1—4 = shan ch'iao (chih) VIII.1—3.

kuśalamūla = dge-ba'i rtsa-ba VIII.16, 17 = shan ken VIII.16

kauśalya = T. mkhas-pa XIX.14,37.

kṣānti = bzod-pa = jen XIX.37.

kṣetra = źiṅ XIX.16, XXII.16, 32 = ch'a (kuo t'u) XIX.16, 32, shih chieh XXII.16.

gati = 'gro-ba = ch'ü XIX.17.

gandharva = dri-za XIX.11—14, 37 = kan t'a p'o XIX.11, 13, 14, 37.

gambhīra = zab-pa XXII 9, 46, zab-mo XIX.37, XXII.36 = (shen) shen XIX.37, XXII.9, 36.

guṇa = T. yon-tan XIX.1, 5, 8, 9, XXII.44 (= varṇa).

ghoṣasamatikrānta = sgra-las śin-tu-'das-pa = kuo yin sheng XXII.10.

ghoṣānugā kṣānti = sgra'i rjes-su-'gro-ba'i bzod-pa = sui shun yin sheng jen XIX.37.

citta = sems XIX.6, 31, 37, XXII.22, 25—27, 29, 31, 43, 47, 48 = $hsin_2$ XIX.31, 37, XXII.22, 25, 27, 29, 43, 48, i $hsiang_2$ XXII.26.

cittabhūmivigama = *bsam-pa'i sa-daṅ-bral-ba* = *kuo hsin ti* XXII.10.
jina = *rgyal-ba* VIII.23, 26, 28, 30, XIX.16, XXII.34 = *fo* XIX.16, 18, 19, 34.
jñāna = *ye-śes* VIII.1—3, 19, XXII.10, 30, 31 = *chih* (*hui*) XIX.22, 30, XXII.31.

tathāgata = *de-bźin-gśegs-pa* VIII.8—10, 12—14, 16, 17, 26, XIX.12, XXII.7, 38 = *ju lai* VIII.8—10, 12—14, 17, XIX.12, XXII.9, 38.

duḥkha = *sdug-bsṅal* XIX.20, 32, 33 = *k'u* XIX 20, 33, *nan* XIX.32.
durgati = *nan-'gro* = *o tao* VIII.16.
deva = *lha* VIII.8, 23, XIX.8, 17, 21, 37, XXII.21 = *t'ien* VIII.8, 17, XIX.17, 37, *hsiu lo* (= *sura*) XXII.21.
devātideva = *lha'i lha* = *t'ien chung chih t'ien* XIX.12.
doṣasamatikrānta = *źe-sdaṅ-las yaṅ-dag-par-'das-pa* = *li chu ch'en* XXII.10.
dharma = *chos* VIII.1—7, 9, 22—24, 27, XIX.1—5, 8, 10, 11, 14, 15, 23, 27, 32, 33, 37, XXII.32, 34, 36, 49, 51 = *fa* VIII.9—12, 14, XIX.1—3, 14, 15, 18, 19, 23, 27, 32, 37, XXII.2, 9—12, 32, 34, 36, 49, 51.
dharmakāya = *chos-kyi sku* XXII.7, 9, 34, 46, 47 = *fa shen* XXII.7, 34, 46, 47.
dhyāna = *bsam-gtan* = *ch'an ting* XIX.35, XXII.16.
[*dhruva*] = *brtan-pa* XXII.10 = *hsin chien ku* XXII.10, *chien shih* (?) XXII.12.

nānātva = *tha-dad* = *chung chung ch'a pieh* XXII.14.
nāma-rūpa = *miṅ-daṅ-gzugs* = *ming se* XXII.22, 25—27.
nāyaka (*vināyaka*) = *'dren-pa* VIII.23, 25, XIX.23 = *fo* XIX.23, *tao shih* XXII.42.
nidhyapti = T. *ṅes-par-rtogs-pa* XIX 14, 15, 37.
nimitta = *mtshan-ma* = $hsiang_1$ XXII.38, 45, 46.
nirabhilāpya = *brjod-med* = XXII.33 = *pu k'o shuo* XXII.10, 33.
nirātmaka = *bdag-med* XIX.30, XXII.6 *wu wo* XIX.30.
[*nirālambana*] = Ch. *li p'an yüan* XXII.12.
[*nirālaya*] = Ch. *li k'u che, wu k'u che* XXII.10.
nirnimitta = *mtshan-ma-med* = *wu chuang mao* XXII.33.
[*nirmāla*] = Ch. *wu kou* XIX.35.
nirvāṇa = *mya-ṅan-las-'das-pa* XXII 11 = *nieh p'an* XXII.12.
nirviśeṣa = *bye-brag-med-pa* XXII.11, 21 = *wu fen ch'i* XXII.9, *wu ch'a i* XXII.21.
nirvṛta = *mya-ṅan-las-'das-(pa)* VIII,31, XIX.23, XXII.11 = *nieh p'an* XIX.23, *mieh* XXII.12.
nirhāra XIX.1, 5, 8, 9 = T. *bsgrub-pa* XIX.5, 9.
niṣparidāha = *yoṅs-su-gduṅ-ba* = *li jo nao, wu jo nao* XXII.12.
[*niṣprapañca*] = Ch. *li hsi lun*, XXII 10, *wu hsi lun* XXII.12.
niḥsvabhāva = *raṅ-bźin-med-pa* XXII.25 = *t'i k'ung* XIX.16.

paramāṇu = *rdul-phran* = (*wei*) *ch'en* XXII 41, 42.
paramārtha = *don dam-pa* XXII.11 = *ti i i ti* XXII.11, 12.
parikarma = *yoṅs-su-sbyoṅ-ba* = *pen yeh* XXII.12.
parinirvṛta = T. *yoṅs-su-mya-ṅan-las-'das* VIII.18.
[*parīkṣita*] = T. *brtags-pa* XXII.11.
pāpa = T. *sdig-pa* XXII.4.
puṅgava = T. *khyu-mchog* VIII.27.
puruṣadamyasārathi VIII 8, 17 = *skyes-bu-'dul-ba'i kha-lo-sgyur-ba* VIII18 = *shih t'iao yü chang fu* VIII.8 17.

prakṛtiviśuddha = T. *rań-bźin-gyis rnam-par-dag-pa* VIII.2.
prajñapti = T. *btags-pa* VIII.11.
pratibhāna = *spobs-pa* = *pien tsai* XIX.30.
[*prapañca*] = Ch. *hsi lun* XXII.12.
prabhāvita = *rab-tu-phye-ba* XXII.7, 46, 47 = *she, hsien hsien* XXII 7, *hsien* (*shih*) XXII.46, 47.
prabhāsvara = *'od-gsal* XXII.14, 22, 27, 49 = *kuang yao* XXII 14, *kuang ming* XXII.22, 49, *kuang chao* XXII.27.

pramāṇa = *tshad* XXII.20, 21, 39, 48, 50—52 = *liang* XXII.21, 39, 48, *hsien lian* XXII.51—52.

bala = *stobs* = *li* XXII.16.
bāla = T. *byis-pa* XXII.4.
buddhi = T. *blo* XXII.9.
(*saṃ*)*bodhi* = *byań-chub* = *p'u t'i* XXII.15, 16, 36.
(*saṃ*)*bodhilakṣaṇa* = *byań-chub-mtshan-ñid* = *p'u t'i hsiang mao* XXII.16.
bodhivaṭa = T. *byań-chub-śiń*.
bodhisatva = *byań-chub-sems-dpa'* VIII.1—3, 19, XIX.1, 3, 4, 6, 10, XXII.1, 3, 7, 8 = *p'u sa* VIII.1, XIX.1, 3. XXII.1, 7, 8.
bhāva = *dńos-po* = *wu* XXII 30, 31.
bhāvanāyoga = *bsgom-pa'i rnal 'byor* VIII 15, 16, XXII.8 = *hsiu hsi* XXII.8.

mahākaruṇā = *sñiń-rje-chen-po* XIX.6 = *ta pei* XXII.12.
mahābhijñā = *mńon-par-śes-pa-chen-po* = *ta shen t'ung* XXII.12.
mahābhijñāna = T. *mńon-par-śes-pa-chen-po* XIX.6.
mahāsatva = *sems-dpa'-chen-po* VIII.1–3, 19, XIX.1, 3, 4, 6, 10, XXII 1, 3, 7, 8 = *mo ho sa* VIII.1, XIX.1, XXII 1, 8.
mānasa = *yid* XIX.25, 31, XXII.30 = *hsin*$_2$ XIX 25, 31, *hsin i* XXII 30.
mārga = *lam* = *tao* XIX.30.
muni = T. *thub-pa* VIII.24, 27.
[*mohasamatikrānta*] = *gti-mug-las-yań-dag-par-'das-pa* = *kuo chu ch'ih* XXII.10.

yathābhūtavacana = *yań-dag-pa-ji-lta-ba'i tshig* = *ju shih yü* XXII.11.
yamalokika = *gśin-rje'i 'jig-rten* = *e kuei* XIX.17.

rāgasamatikrānta = *'dod-chags-las-yań-dag-par-'das-pa* = *kuo chu yü* XXII 10.
rūpakāya = *gzugs-kyi sku* = *se shen* XXII.7, 34, 39.

lakṣaṇa = *mtshan* XXII.15, 19, 22, 25 = *hsiang*$_1$ XXII.19, 20, 22, 25, *hsiang chuang mao* XXII.15.
lokadhātu = *'jig-rten-gyi khams* VIII.11, 25, XXII.40 = *shih chieh* VIII.10, 11 XXII.40.
lokanātha = *'jig-rten-mgon-po* XXII.13, 17, 23, 42, 54 = *shih men ts'in* XXII.13, 23, *shih ts'in* XXII.17, 54.
lokanāyaka = T. *'jig-rten-'dren-pa* XXII.18.
lokavid VIII.8, 17, XIX.22 = *'jig-rten-mkhyen-pa* VIII.8, *'jig-rten-rig-pa* XIX.22 = *shih men chieh* VIII.8, 17.

varṇa = *kha-dog* XXII.12, 18, 45 = *se* XXII.18, 44, 45.

vikurvita = *rnam-thar-sprul-pa* = *shen t'ung* XXII.19.
vijñāna = *rnam-śes* = *hsin₂* XXII.31.
vidyācaraṇasampanna VIII.8, 17 = *rig-pa-daṅ-źabs-su-ldan-pa* VIII.8 = *ming hsing tsu* VIII.8, 17.
vinipāta = T. *log-par-lhuṅ-ba* VIII 16, 29.
vipañcita = *rnam-(par)-spros-pa* VIII. 7, XIX.1, 4, 5, 8, 10, 14 = *wu hsi lun* VIII.14.
vipāka = *rnam-par-smin-pa* = *kuo pao* XXII.22.
vimati = *yid gñis* = *i₃* XIX.35.
vimukta = *rnam-par-grol* XXII.30, 31 = *c'hi she* XXII.30, *chieh t'o* XXII.31.
vimokṣa = *rnam-thar* = *chieh t'o* XXII.16.
viraja = T. *rdul-bral* VIII.27, 28.
vilakṣana = T. *mtshan-ñid-mi-'dra* XIX.16.
viśeṣa = *bye-brag* = *hsiang₁* XXII.45.
visabhāga = *skal-(pa)-mi-mñam* XIX.16, 26 = *lei ming pu t'ung* XXII.25.
vedanā = *tshor-ba* = *shou* XIX.20.
vyāhārā = *tha-sñad* = *yen₂ shuo, shih su* XXII.11.

śatapuṇyanirjāta = *bsod-nams-brgya-pa-las-skyes-pa* = *wu liang fu te chih so ch'u sheng* XXII.9.
śānta = *źi-ba* VIII.6, 30, XXII.11, 23 = *chi mieh* XXII.11, 23.
śāstar VIII.8, 17, XXII.21 = *ston-pa* VIII.8, XXII.21 = *shih* VIII.8, 17.
śītala = *bsil-ba* = *ts'ing liang* XXII.12.
śīla = *tshul-khrims* = *chiai* XIX.35.
śūnya(ka) = *stoṅ-pa* VIII.2, 6, XIX.30, XXII.6= *k'ung* XIX.30, *k'ung chi*(?) XXII.22.

saṃketa = *brda* = *ho hui* XXII.11.
saṃjñā = *'du-śes* = *hsiang₂* XIX.25, XXII.26—28.
samatā = *mñam-pa-ñid* VIII.7, XIX.1, 4, 5, 8, 10, 14, 34=*p'ing teng* VIII.14, XIX.34.
samādhi = *tiṅ-ṅe-'dzin* VIII 1, 4, 14—16, 19, 28—30, XIX.1, 4, 5, 8, 10, 14, 27, XXII.1, 3, 7, 8, 13, 14, 23, 24 = *san mei* VIII.14, 15, XIX.1, 27, XXII.8, 13, 24, *ting* XXII.23, 24.
samāhita = *mñam-par-bźag-pa* = *k'ung chi*(?) XXII.22.
[*sarvadarśanasamatikrānta*] =Ch. *kuo chu chien* XXII.10.
sarvanimittavibhāvita = *mtshan-ma-thams-cad rnam-par-bśig-pa* = *li chu hsiang* XXII.9.
sarvanimittāpagata = *mtshan-ma-thams-cad-daṅ-bral-ba* = *li chu hsiang* XXII.9.
sarvaprapañcasamatikrānta=T. *spros-pa-thams-cad-las yaṅ-dag-par-'das-pa* XXII.10.
[*sarvavipākasamatikrānta*] = Ch. *li chu pao* XXII.10.
sāmānya = *mtshuṅs-par-'gyur-ba* = *t'ung ssŭ hsiang* XXII.11.
sāraga = *sñiṅ-po* = *hsin chien ku* (?) XXII.10.
sukha = *dga'-ba* XIX.21, *bde-ba* XXII.4 = *k'uai lo* XIX.21.
sukhadukhāviprakampya = *bde-ba-daṅ-sdug-bsṅal-gyis mi-bskyod-pa* = *wu tung chuan* (= *viprakampya*) XXII.10.
sugata VIII.7, 8, 17 = *bde-bar-gśegs-pa* VIII.7, 8 = *shan shih* VIII.8, 17.
[*supratiṣṭhita*] = Ch. *shan an chu* XXII.9.
[*sūkṣma*] = Ch. *wei hsi* XXII.12.
svabhāva = *raṅ-bźin* VIII.7, XIX.1, 4, 5, 8, 10, 14, 27, XXII.31, *ṅo-bo-ñid* VIII.1—3, 7 = *t'i sheng* VIII.14, XXII.31.

LIST OF THE CHINESE WORDS
OCCURRING IN THE TEXT
(cf. the Table which follows).

1. a nou to lo
2. a seng chih
3. an shi kao
4. ch'a (kuo t'u)
5. ch'an (ting)
6. chi mieh
7. chia
8. chia sha
9. chisi
10. chiao shih chia
11. chieh
12. chieh t'o
13. chien cheng chi
14. chien shih
15. chih
16. chih (hui)
17. ch'i she
18. ch'ih
19. cho chia p'o lo
20. chu
21. chung
22. chung chung ch'a pieh
23. ch'u li sheng ti
24. ch'ü
25. e kuei
26. fa
27. fa shen
28. fan
29. fen pieh
30. fen shih
31. fo
32. fo ch'u shih
33. fu
34. han ping
35. heng ho
36. ho hui
37. hung tzŭ
38. huo chiao jo
39. hsi lun
40. hsiang$_1$
41. hsiang$_2$
42. hsiang chuang mao
43. hsien hsien
44. hsien liang
45. hsien shih
46. hsin$_1$
47. hsin$_2$
48. hsin i
49. hsin chien ku
50. hsiu hsi
51. hsiu lo
52. hsü i
53. hsü mi
54. i$_1$
55. i$_2$
56. i$_3$
57. i$_4$
58. i chung sheng
59. i hsiang$_1$
60. i hsiang$_2$
61. i hsin (an) chu
62. i i
63. i shih
64. jen
65. ju lai
66. ju shih yü
67. kan t'a p'o
68. ku
69. k'u
70. k'uai lo
71. kuang chao
72. kuang ming
73. kuang yao
74. k'ung
75. k'ung chi
76. kuo
77. kuo chu chien
78. kuo chu ch'ih
79. kuo chu pao
80. kuo chu yü
81. kuo hsin ti
82. kuo pao
83. kuo yin sheng
84. lei ming pu t'ung
85. li
86. li chu ch'en
87. li chu hsiang
88. li hsi lun
89. li jo nao
90. li k'u che
91. li neng
92. li p'an yüan
93. li yen yin
94. liang
95. liu li ts'in
96. mieh
97. mieh hsi lun i ku
98. ming hsing tsu
99. ming se

100. mo
101. mo ho sa
102. mu chen ling t'o
103. nan
104. nan liang
105. nan ssŭ
106. nieh p'an
107. o tao
108. pan che shih ch'i
109. pen yeh
110. (pien) chai
111. pien man
112. pien tsai
113. p'ing teng
114. po hsün
115. pu chu
116. pu fei pang
117. pu huai
118. pu k'o chien
119. pu (k'o) ssŭ (i)
120. pu k'o shu
121. pu k'o shuo
122. pu shan
123. p'u sa
124. p'u t'i
125. san mei
126. san mei ching t'ien
127. se
128. se shen
129. su_1
130. su_2
131. sui
132. sui chun yin sheng jen
133. sung
134. ssŭ wei ta pei
135. shan
136. shan an chu
137. shan ch'iao (chih)
138. shan ken
139. shan ssŭ i
140. shan shih
141. she
142. shen
143. shen hsin
144. shen hsin ts'ing tsing
145. shen li
146. shen shen
147. shen t'ung
148. sheng
149. shih
150. shih chieh
151. shih liu hsün
152. shih men chieh
153. shih men ts'in
154. shih sien kung
155. shih su
156. shih t'iao yü chang fu
157. shih tsun
158. shou
159. shuo shih i ch'ieh chu fa t'i hsing p'ing teng wu hsi lun san mei
160. ta pei
161. ta mu chen
162. ta chen t'ung
163. t'a kuang shuo
164. tan yen shuo
165. tao
166. te ch'i pien
167. te tzŭ yu tzŭ tsai li ku
168. ti i i ti
169. ti shih
170. t'i hsing
171. t'i k'ung
172. t'ien
173. t'ien chung chih t'ien
174. ting
175. tu_1
176. tu_2
177. t'ung ssŭ hsiang
178. ts'in
179. ts'ing liang
180. ts'ing tsing
181. ts'u ta
182. tzŭ shen
183. wei ch'en
184. wei hsi
185. wu
186. wu ch'a i
187. wu ch'ang
188. wu ch'iung chi
189. wu (chu) lou
190. wu chuang mao
191. wu chü chu
192. wu fen ch'i
193. wu hsi
194. wu hsi lun
195. wu hsien
196. wu (hsien) liang
197. wu jo nai
198. wu kou (hsin)
199. wu k'u che
200. wu liang fu te chih so ch'u sheng ju lai shuo yü i i
201. wu neng ssŭ
202. wu neng sheng
203. wu neng ts'ü
204. wu p'o huai
205. wu p'o huai i chien shih ku
206. wu so i
207. wu so yu ch'i
208. wu shang
209. wu shu
210. wu tung chuan
211. wu tung yao
212. wu tsin
213. wa tso
214. wu ts'ü chu
215. wu wo
216. wu yu erh wei i hsiang ku
217. wu (yu) fen pieh
218. wu yu huai
219. wu (yu) hsiang
220. wu yu hsien ch'i
221 wu (yu) p'ien (chi)
222 wu yu sheng
223. wu yu wei ch'en shuo wei hsi ku
224. wu yü
225. yeh
226. yen shuo
227. yen_2 shuo
228. ying (kung)
229. yu hsi shen li
230. yu hsi shuo
231. yu yin sheng i ssŭ hsiang ku
232. yüeh kuang
233. yüeh teng san mei ching

1 阿 耨 多 羅
2 阿 僧 祇
3 安 世 高
4 刹 國 土
5 禪 定
6 寂 滅
7 加
8 袈 裟
9 戒
10 憍 尸 迦
11 劫
12 解 脫
13 堅 正 智
14 堅 實
15 值
16 智 慧
17 棄 捨
18 持
19 斫 迦 婆 羅
20 著
21 種
22 種 種 差 別
23 出 離 聲 地
24 趣
25 餓 鬼
26 法
27 法 身
28 梵
29 分 別
30 糞 屎
31 佛
32 佛 出 世
33 福
34 寒 氷
35 恒 河
36 和 會
37 紅 紫
38 火 焦 熱
39 戲 論
40 相
41 想
42 相 狀 貌
43 顯 現
44 限 量
45 顯 示
46 信
47 心
48 心 憶
49 心 堅 固
50 修 習
51 修 羅
52 宿 業
53 須 彌
54 以
55 義
56 疑
57 異
58 一 衆 生
59 一 相
60 憶 想
61 一 心 安 住
62 一 義
63 一 時
64 忍
65 如 來
66 如 實 語
67 乾 闥 婆
68 故
69 苦
70 快 樂
71 光 照
72 光 明
73 光 曜
74 空
75 空 寂
76 果
77 過 諸 見
78 過 諸 癡
79 過 諸 報
80 過 諸 欲
81 過 心 地
82 果 報
83 過 音 聲
84 類 名 不 同

85 力
86 離 諸 瞋
87 離 諸 相
88 離 戲 論
89 離 熱 惱
90 離 窟 宅
91 力 能
92 離 攀 緣
93 離 言 音
94 量
95 琉 璃 琴
96 滅
97 滅戲論義故
98 明 行 足
99 名 色
100 魔
101 摩 訶 薩
102 目 真 隣 陀
103 難
104 難 量
105 難 思
106 涅 槃
107 惡 道
108 般遮尸棄
109 本 業
110 遍 窄
111 遍 滿
112 辯 才
113 平 等
114 波 旬
115 不 著
116 不 誹 謗
117 不 壞
118 不 可 見
119 不 可 思 議
120 不 可 數
121 不 不 可 說
122 不 善
123 菩 薩
124 菩 提
125 三 昧
126 三 昧 經 典
127 色
128 色 身
129 蘇
130 酥
131 雖
132 隨 順 音 聲 忍
133 誦
134 思 惟 大 悲
135 禪
136 善 安 住
137 善 巧 知
138 善 根
139 善 思 義
140 善 逝
141 攝
142 身
143 深 信
144 深 信 清 淨
145 神 力
146 甚 深
147 神 通
148 生
149 師
150 世 界
151 十 六 句
152 世 門 解
153 世 門 親
154 釋 先 公
155 世 俗
156 士 調御丈夫、
157 世 尊
158 受
159 說是一切諸法
體性平等無戲
論三昧
160 大 悲
161 大 日 真
162 大 神 通
163 他 廣 說
164 但 言 說
165 道
166 得 其 便

167 得自由自在力故
168 第一義諦
169 帝釋
170 體性
171 體空
172 天
173 天中之天
174 定
175 讀
176 覩
177 同思想
178 親
179 清涼
180 清淨
181 鹿大
182 自身
183 微塵
184 微細
185 物
186 無差異
187 無常
188 無窮極
189 無諸漏
190 無狀貌
191 無居處
192 無分齊
193 無戲
194 無戲論
195 無限
196 無限量
197 無熱惱
198 無垢心
199 無窟宅
200 無量福德之所出生如來說於一義
201 無能思
202 無能勝
203 無能取
204 無破壞
205 無破壞以堅實故
206 無所依
207 無所有起
208 無上
209 無數
210 無動轉
211 無動搖
212 無盡
213 無作
214 無取著
215 無我
216 無有二惟一相故
217 無有分別
218 無有壞
219 無有相
220 無有限齊
221 無有邊際
222 無有生
223 無有微塵說微細故
224 五欲
225 業
226 演說
227 言說
228 應供
229 遊戲神力
230 又細說
231 有音聲以思想故
232 月光
233 月燈三昧經

CORRIGENDA

Page	*line*	*instead of*	*read*
5	12	Conmmentary	Commentary
6	4	Orientalla	Orientalia
8	24	*'pags*	*'phags*
10	10 and 21	*An shi kao*	*An shih kao*
12	10 from below	vasriety	variety
13	5 ,, ,,	vesre	verse
14	16 ,, ,,	form	forms
15	9	*śrūtva*	*śrutva*
25	17 from below	*Śrīmālādevīsiṃhanandaº*	*Śrīmālādevīsiṃhanādaº*
25	3 ,, ,,	Sidhi	Siddhi
76	3 ,, ,,	*liu li ts'in*	*liu li ch'ín*
78	4 ,, ',	*pien tse*	*pien chai*
79	1 ,, ,,	*hsü i*	*hsü yeh*
92	12 fr. bel. and 6 fr. below	*saṃñjā*	*saṃjñā*
93	6 from below	*po sun*	*po hsün*
102	16 ,, ,,	*pan che shih chia*	*pan che shih ch'i*
102	10 ,, ,,	*ling*	*lin*
103	19 fr. bel. and 4 fr. bel.	*p'ien*	*pien*
105	17	*hsin chien ku*	*chien cheng chih*
108	Nº 9	*chisi*	*chiai*
108	Nº 52	*hsü i*	*hsü yeh*
108	Nº 95	*liu li ts'in*	*liu li ch'in*
108	Nº 102	*ling*	*lin*
109	Nº 126	*t'ien*	*tien*
109	Nº 132	*chun*	*shun*
109	Nº 162	*chen*	*shen*
109	Nº 221	*p'ien*	*pien*